Whistling Past
the Graveyard

Whistling Past the Graveyard

Selected Short Stories

by

Peter Sellers

For Adrienne,
Keep Whistling!
All the Best,

Mosaic Press
Oakville, ON — Niagara Falls, NY

Canadian Cataloguing in Publication Data

Sellers, Peter, 1956-
        Whistling past the graveyard: selected short stories

Crime Mystery/Fantasy.
ISBN 0-88962-661-8

I. Titles.

PS8587.E437W44 1999   C813'.54   C99-931539-0
PR9199.3.S387W44 1999

No part of this book may be reproduced or transmitted in any form, by any means, electronic or mechanical, including photocopying and recording information storage and retrieval systems, without permission in writing from the publisher, except by a reviewer who may quote brief passages in a review.

Published by MOSAIC PRESS, P.O. Box 1032, Oakville, Ontario, L56 5E9, Canada. Offices and warehouse at 1252 Speers Road, Units #1&2, Oakville, Ontario, L6L 5N9, Canada and Mosaic Press, 4500 Witmer Industrial Estates, PMB 145, Niagara Falls, NY 14305-1386

Mosaic Press acknowledges the assistance of the Canada Council, and the Department of Canadian Heritage for their support of our publishing programme.

Copyright © 1999 Peter Sellers
ISBN 0-88962-661-8
Printed and bound in Canada

THE CANADA COUNCIL   LE CONSEIL DES ARTS
FOR THE ARTS   DU CANADA
SINCE 1957   DEPUIS 1957

MOSAIC PRESS, in Canada:
1252 Speers Road, Units #1&2,
Oakville, Ontario, L6L 5N9
Phone / Fax: 905-825-2130
cp507@freenet.toronto.on.ca

MOSAIC PRESS, in the USA:
4500 Witmer Industrial Estates
PMB 145, Niagara Falls, NY
14305-1386
Tel:1-800-387-8992
cp507@freenet.toronto.on.ca

Acknowledgements

Back in the early eighties, I was writing stories that no one wanted to buy. They were pseudo-British sex farces inspired by the likes of Kingsley Amis and Tom Sharpe. I complained about this lack of success to Rochelle Kahn and she gave me the most sage advice I've ever received. "Why don't you write something someone will want to buy?" It was a lamp in the darkness.

I wrote a crime story, still pseudo-British, and sold it to *Mike Shayne Mystery Magazine* for a promised 1 ½ cents per word. "Loss of a Faculty" appeared in the July, 1984, issue. I sent them a second story, called "A Difference of Degree" (which is included in this book as "Boogie Man") and they published that, too, in August, 1985. Then the magazine folded. I never got my 1 ½ cents per word for either story, but I did get my start.

Thanks to Rochelle for her advice and for helping clarify the endings of a couple of the earlier stories. To Charles Fritch for accepting those first two stories when he was editor of MSMM. To Don Hutchison who helped me by rejecting a couple of these stories until I fixed them and to Janet Hutchings for bringing me in to *Ellery Queen Mystery Magazine*. Thanks to Edward D. Hoch, James Powell, William Bankier, Gregory Ward, Robert J. Sawyer, Peter Robinson, Eric Wright and especially Ted Wood - all writers I respect and who have helped me in ways they may not even realize. And to Howard Aster for his support and encouragement since 1987.

Belated thanks to Marv Lachman, who helped me out considerably several years ago in compiling a collection of Bill Bankier stories, and who I neglected to acknowledge at that time.

On a more personal note, thanks and love to Daniel and Jennifer, constant sources of wonderment.

Finally, thanks to Leslie Watts for helping me understand that less is more.

Peter Sellers
Toronto, 1999

To

Bob Walkinshaw
Ann Taylor
Stewart Bull
Bob Simmons

who taught me well - with respect and gratitude.

Introduction

Weekend package trips to Hell.
A hunter of human heads.
A lover's bed wired to execute.

Welcome to the offbeat world of Peter Sellers. No, not the actor who stumbled through all those Pink Panther movies as the ineffectual Inspector Clouseau. Not *that* Peter Sellers. Not the dead one. *This* Peter Sellers doesn't do pratfalls. This one writes stories. As you are about to find out, he writes sharp, lively stories filled with satiric wit and clever twists.

Unlike his actor namesake — who, as we speak, is still dead — this Peter is a relatively young guy, early-fortyish, with close-cropped hair, a neat full beard, and a wicked twinkle in his eyes as well as in his word processor. He's smart enough to know that crime doesn't pay — at least not enough — so he's a freelance advertising writer by day and a crime writer by night.

Because many of his stories have appeared in *Ellery Queen Mystery, Alfred Hitchcock Mystery,* and the late lamented *Mike Shayne Mystery* magazines and because he is well known as the prize-winning creator and editor of Canada's prestigious *Cold Blood* anthologies, Sellers is thought of primarily as a mystery writer, but his work ranges beyond that narrow definition. I'm pleased to note that two of the stories herein appeared in my own *Northern Frights* fantasy series and that both contain more than a dollop of dark humor.

Perhaps it's late night inspiration that produces work like "The Vampires Next Door," concerning the apartment dweller whose new neighbours turn out to be more experienced blood-suckers than his landlord. It's a very funny story, but just when you think that's all it is, it takes an abrupt turn into Stephen King territory. (Did I forget to mention that Peter writes ad copy for a local funeral home?)

So where does a writer get these ideas? Harlan Ellison used to say that he sent away for them to a post office box in New Jersey, but the truth is that ideas are the stock and trade of the short story biz. Sellers admits that he was greatly inspired by the black-and-white noir movies of the forties and fifties with stars like Dick Powell and Robert Mitchum, and by writers like Raymond Chandler and John D. MacDonald who, with under-stated skill and economy, told stories about tough guys on both sides of the law.

You can see all of these influences in Peter's work, but there's a lot more as well. If the juxtapositions of humour, crime, sus-pense and satire seem at first unrelated, there is a common thread that ties his work together. When questioned, he admits readily that most of his stories, whether humorous or deadly serious, are about love gone wrong. The book's title story, for instance, is a paranoid vision worthy of suspense master Cornell Woolrich. Like those of Woolrich, Sellers' characters live in a world in which dreams do not come true and plans seldom work out — lives subverted by what Anthony Boucher once described as a sense of "the everyday gone wrong."

In the old days most crime stories were labeled "whodun-nits," based on the assumption that they involved detective he-roes solving mysteries. Sellers works a modern vein involving unromantic acceptance of the banality of evil in everyday life. It's a corrupt old world, his stories suggest, requiring the hatching of mundane criminous endeavours. Many, if not all, of these schemes get screwed up woefully by all-too human characters beguiled into desperate stratagems. In the course of a typical Sellers story there is usually one bad decision made, and on that hangs the plot — as well as the perpetrator.

So welcome to the offbeat world of Peter Sellers. The tour begins with "Freak Attraction," the author's own take on one of the smallest of all fiction genres, Carnival Noir. It's the one about the Siamese twins, the knife-throwing dwarf, and the Snake Woman who... Oh, forget it. Just turn the page. Read the story.

Enjoy.

Don Hutchison

Contents

Freak Attraction

Gilroy was desperate for another woman with four legs like the one he'd discovered in Quebec back in 1918. Either that or another Jo-Jo the Dog-Faced Boy. He'd even settle for someone like The Zebra Man - who he'd heard was causing a stir in England - with two-inch wide black stripes tattooed all over his body.

"Somewhere on this god damn planet," Gilroy said, "there's got to be god damn freak nobody's seen before." They were walking past the geek pit and Gilroy stopped, spat and pointed. "Look at this." He poked Alfred sharply in the chest and then jabbed his finger at the canvas enclosure that housed the geek. "A god damn geek pit. I'm reduced to a god damn geek pit. Me. The Great God Damn Gilroy." He shook his head and started off again towards the midway. Alfred had to trot to keep up.

They walked past the bannerline for the Ten-In-One show. Huge lurid images on the posters exaggerated the attractions the marks could expect to find inside. Alfred was looking at them as he walked and he almost bumped into Gilroy who had stopped again. This time Gilroy pointed at the posters.

"What have I got?" Gilroy asked. "Tell me that. What have I got?"

Alfred didn't bother answering. He'd learned from experience.

"I'll tell you what I've got," Gilroy ploughed on. "I've got a couple of pin heads. I've got a knife-throwing dwarf. A bunch of singing midgets who couldn't carry a tune in a basket. I've got a bearded lady. God damn it, everybody's got a bearded lady.

"And what am I up against? I'm up against Johnny Eck. I'm up against the god damn Hilton Sisters playing the piano and dancing with guys in tuxedos. I'm up against those god damn Ubangis with lips out to here." He held his hands about two feet from his face which Alfred knew, from having seen the Ubangis, was something of an exaggeration. But then, exaggeration was one of Gilroy's long suits.

"It was easier back thirty years ago, even twenty, when the rubes would buy anything and it was all new. We could throw anything in front of 'em and talk it up and they'd buy it. And what we couldn't find we'd gaff up. I remember once taking two field hands from Alabama, throwing wigs and bone necklaces on 'em and - hey presto! - I had two cannibals from an island of the Antipodes. The rubes ate it up. They didn't know. They didn't care. I'll tell you, Alfred, we live in cynical times. Cynical god damn times, young man."

Alfred had been with Gilroy six months. He'd joined because Gilroy was one of the greats in the pantheon of freak showmen. Barnum, C.W. Coup, Clyde Ingalls, Farini, Gilroy. They were the legends and Alfred wanted to learn from the best.

He'd joined the show as a roustabout and jack - of - all trades but when Slim Maxwell, the outside talker, dropped dead of a stroke one afternoon in the midwest, Alfred was pressed into service. He'd been doing it ever since, standing outside the tent by the bally platform. Selling it to the rubes. Getting them in. Getting as many of them as he could to part with one thin dime.

"Inside for the insignificant sum of one dime, two nickels, ten coppers - that's right, for the tenth part of a dollar, the price of a shave, sir, or a piece of brightly coloured ribbon, madam - you can behold the greatest, most awe inspiring aggregation of human marvels and monstrosities ever gathered together in one single edifice. In fact, at laying your eyes on these astounding anomalies you may well ask yourselves - are they human or monsters or something in between?"

Alfred knew all the stories about Gilroy. He'd been in the freak show business for forty years. He'd run a dime museum in Chicago and another in New York. He'd worked with Barnum. He'd helped arrange the wedding of General Tom Thumb and Lavinia Warren. He'd toured Europe with them and been introduced to royalty. He credited himself with the discovery of Captain Costentenus and his heavily tattooed torso. He had pioneered the Circassian beauty fad, the popularity of cannibals and more limbless wonders than he could count on any number of hands and feet.

He was a master opportunist. One day in Saskatchewan, short one exhibit, Gilroy spotted a really tall man in the audience. After the show, Gilroy walked up to the rube. "Hey," he said, "how'd you like to be a giant?" The next week, decked out in high-heeled western boots and what must have been a twenty-gallon hat, Jack Thompson from Saskatoon was paraded in front of audiences as Treetop Thompson - The Man So Tall He Has To Bend Down To Let The Moon Go By.

But that was some time ago. In the past few years, things had turned sour for Gilroy. His fabled ability to find or fabricate exotic freaks seemed to desert him. The publicity stunts he came up with, which had worked without exception for decades, no longer always panned out as planned. Alfred thought about a recent example. Gilroy had a pair of Siamese twins that had travelled with his show for several years. They had always been presented to audiences as leading normal, happy lives. Married to normal wives. Blessed with normal children who would join them on occasion and appeared in the post-card photographs the twins sold from the stage. The picture of contentment.

The reality, however, differed wildly from the presentation. For Chung and Zeng hated one another. There had always been tension between them but it exploded into open animosity when, six weeks after their joint wedding, Chung discovered that his wife and Zeng had been carrying on a torrid affair behind Chung's back. The two men barely spoke and the words they exchanged were often heated and bitter. Gilroy decided to exploit this rage.

He had the two men fitted out with boxing gloves.

"It's perfect," Gilroy said. "We'll have 'em duke it out. We'll have a referee. Strictly Marquis of Queensbury. But they can't run away. And just one of them can't be knocked down. So there'll never be a loser. This could play for years."

In the end, it played for about two minutes. The one time Chung and Zeng fought, the sideshow tent was jammed with people. Gilroy at the edge of the crowd, full of his own brilliance. Then the fight started. Unable to dodge blows or step back to reduce the impact, the twins pummelled each other mercilessly. The blood flew, spattering the crowd nearest the stage. When they drew back in horror and disgust, there was no room, so tightly packed was the crowd. Panic started to swell in the tent as people scrambled for the exit. Sensing total disaster, Gilroy yelled at the referee to stop the fight. But when the ref stepped in to break things up, one of the pugilists - debate still raged as to whether it was Chung or Zeng - hit him very hard on the side of the head, breaking his jaw. Finally both fighters collapsed and spent the next three weeks in hospital.

So now, as he did every day, Gilroy was striding along the midway with Alfred in tow, praying aloud for one of nature's mistakes to fall into his lap.

The crowd that day was small. Alfred was talking himself hoarse. The shills were coming up in full force, pretending to be real customers excited about the prospect of what lay inside. And yet, as was the case now more often than not, the tent was half full at best. And most of the rubes came to watch the geek.

That night after counting the receipts, which seemed to take less time every day, Gilroy sat in his trailer office with Alfred and Laszlo, an old-time carny who'd shared the good times with Gilroy and was now sharing a bottle of bootleg whiskey.

There was a knock on the door. "Yeah?" Gilroy called. "Come in." He didn't bother hiding the booze. He'd been bribing cops off and on for four decades.

The door opened and a woman came in. She was tall and slender but she moved in a way that made her seem all curves.

Gilroy, Laszlo and Alfred looked at her in some surprise. Alfred had never seen her before and, judging from their reactions, the others hadn't either. Nobody said anything right away and Alfred felt an involuntary tightening in his throat. He couldn't see her face. He didn't imagine any of the three of them could; her head was above the circle of light from the desk lamp and so hidden in shadow. But there was something about her that made it difficult for him to draw breath.

"What can we do for you, little lady?" Gilroy asked finally.

She spoke softly. "I understand that you are seeking a new attraction."

"And where might you have heard that?"

"Word circulates," she said.

"It does that," Gilroy agreed. "So, do you happen to know where we can find one?"

"Yes, I do." And she stepped fully into the light. Her face was lean and slightly sharp, dark hair cut short like a cap on her skull. Her eyes were an unusual colour, a greenish yellow that shouldn't have looked healthy but did. She stared at the three men and did not seem to blink for a very long time.

"Well," Gilroy said after waiting for some seconds, "tell me about this fabulous freak you've got for me."

But she didn't tell them. She opened her mouth and showed them.

"Holy Mary," Gilroy said. And Laszlo crossed himself.

"No expense has been spared - no hardship gone unendured - in our untiring efforts to bring you this exhilarating and edifying ensemble. We have personally travelled to the farthest reaches of the globe, paddled by open canoe to the uncharted headwaters of the teeming Amazon, navigated the rocky shoals of the outer Antipodes, scoured countless remote hamlets and distant villages, to personally guarantee that what you see today will be unlike anything you've ever witnessed before."

"Where do you think she came from?" Alfred asked.

Gilroy made a dismissive motion with his hand. "Who cares where she came from? She's here. That's what counts."

"Do you think it's real? It could be make-up or something."

"Kid, I've been around gaffed freaks all my life. I can smell the fakes a mile off. She's the genuine article all right. She's one honest - to - god freak." He smiled widely, thinking about it. "The rubes are going to

5

go for her in a big way, kid. You just watch the Great Gilroy work his magic."

~

Alfred tapped softly on the door of the trailer. Hoping that she wasn't inside or that if she was she wouldn't hear him. Gilroy had given her temporary use of the trailer that had belonged to the Human Skeleton, a lecherous old man who had caught pneumonia and died a month before. Alfred waited several seconds. He heard no movement inside the trailer and was about to turn away when her voice came through the door.

"Yes?"

The voice wasn't loud but it startled him. "Hi. It's Alfred, I was in with Mr. Gilroy and..."

"Yes. I recognize your voice. The door is not locked."

Alfred reached for the door handle, then drew his hand back and wiped the palm on his pant leg. He opened the door and went in. It was dim inside the trailer and he didn't see the woman at first.

"Over here," she said. He turned to his left and he could make her out dimly, curled up on the cot. "Can I help you with anything?"

Alfred looked at her vague outline, perfectly still. He could not distinguish her mouth. "Mr. Gilroy just asked me to come and see if there was anything you needed."

"I'm fine, thank you."

"Do you want anything to eat? I can have the cook whip something up."

"Thank you, but I'm not hungry just now."

"Okay, then. Oh, and Mr. Gilroy wanted me to say that they need to get a costume together for you and work out a few details - you know, about money and how to present you - and he reckons you should be in the show by the weekend."

"Thank you. And please tell Mr. Gilroy that I won't appear on the bally."

"No. I don't think he'd want that anyway. Good night."

"Good night," she said. "Sleep well."

Alfred shut the trailer door behind him, and all he could think about was how still she sat.

～

For the next three days, Gilroy was like a young boy. He walked around the carnival with an unfamiliar spring in his step. Talking to himself. Laughing at private jokes. And, in a sealed tent at the far end of the midway, he had painters working in secret on an addition to the bannerline.

Finally, he called Alfred and Laszlo together with his other attractions and said, "This is it."

All the freaks were there. Hugo, the knife thrower. The Whitney midgets. Seymour and Chloe, the pinheads. Sweet Adeline, the bearded lady. Everybody except the new star.

"Ladies and gentlemen," Gilroy began, "I present to you our latest attraction. Something never before seen. Something of neither heaven nor earth. Neither human nor beast."

"Knock it off, Gilroy," Hugo said. "We're not a bunch of rubes here. Give us the straight skinny."

"Yes, of course you're not. In my enthusiasm I got carried away. Here she is. Eva. Born of Eve. Sired by the serpent." He waved his arm, and one of the painters pulled a rope, and the covering dropped away from the new banner. "Half Woman, Half Serpent," the bold script shouted from the top. And there she was. Her legs were not shown in the picture. Instead her body ended in a serpent's tail. Her arms beckoned toward the audience. Her mouth was open.

Everyone just looked at the painting for a moment, then Hugo snorted dismissively. "They shouldn't call you the Great Gilroy," he said. "They should call you the Great Hyperbole."

The rest of the freaks laughed but Alfred thought that the painters had got it just about right.

～

When Alfred was eight years old, his father took him to a sideshow. Outside the tent, he'd been enraptured by the garish images on the bannerline and mesmerised by the patter of the talker. Inside, he'd watched an armless man cut out a string of paper dolls with a pair of scissors clenched between his toes. He had been at once attracted and repelled. But he begged his father to take him back to every sideshow that passed through their town. When he was old enough, he went himself. Always with the same feeling: a strong desire to stop looking and an utter inability to do so.

The attraction grew over time, drawing him to visit sideshows with increasing frequency. Then to follow them. He became a connoisseur, seeking out the best and the most exotic. And then the idea grew in him that he could be a showman. That he could spend his life among the freaks. That was when he went to work for Gilroy.

～

"You see, son," Gilroy explained to Alfred one day early on, "freaks are not born, they're made. Let me tell you a story. Once, way back about 1915, 1916, I came across this Mexican fellow. He was an itinerant labourer, picked lettuce, oranges, whatever was in season, and there wasn't much unusual about him except that he had this huge thing growing on his forehead. A big god damn growth, like this." Gilroy held his hands up in front of his face and mimed a round growth, about the size of a small grapefruit, just above his eyes. "I don't know if it was a tumour or a boil or what, but it was substantial. Anyway, it was all covered over with hair. So we shaved some of the hair off it, used a little make-up and paint, and put a face on it. I don't suspect the god damn thing looked very real but it didn't matter. The rubes came out in droves to see the

Remarkable Two-Headed Man. See, it wasn't what he was, it was what we made him out to be. That's what people bought. They wanted to see a two-headed man. And what we gave them was close enough. We toured Miguel for about three years straight, then one day we found him dead in his trailer. I think that thing on his head killed him, but I'll tell you he was a trouper. A great god damn freak. Haven't had a good two-headed man since."

"In the past, in this very tent, we have shown you the missing link - neither man nor beast, but halfway between. But today, ladies and gentlemen, included for the price of one thin dime, you will be the very first to see an attraction so spectacular, so unsettling, so awe-inspiring that your understanding of the world may never be the same again. Not halfway between man and beast, but halfway between heaven and hell. Eva. The daughter of Eve. But not the daughter of Adam. Half woman, half serpent. A woman unevolved since Eden."

Eva was a hit from the word Go. The first day, the crowds weren't any bigger than they had been the day before. But for the first time Alfred could recall, they were transfixed. He saw this when he slipped away from his spot outside the tent and ducked inside for a moment. Traffic by that point was light, and he didn't figure on missing too many marks if he took a quick peek.

Eva wore a suit that hugged her body, emphasising her leanness and the undulating way that she moved. It was the kind of outfit that would not be tolerated in public but that sideshows had been getting away with for years under the guise of presentations made in the name of science.

But what riveted attention was not Eva's slim body but, as Alfred knew it would be, her mouth.

He saw it in the men's faces the instant Eva opened her lips and her tongue weaved out. It darted back and forth an impossible distance beyond her lips. The forked tip flicked up and down with blurring speed, and then it waved back and forth in a sensuous rhythm, long and forked and tasting the air. Sensing about like a snake's, for danger or for prey.

At first, Alfred watched as spellbound as everyone else, although he had already seen it many times before. Then he forced himself to turn away and look at the crowd. He recognized on the men's faces the same mixture of desire and revulsion that he felt in himself. He watched as they pushed their straw hats back and mopped their brows. Licked their lips. Tugged at collars and loosened ties. Their gaze never wavering from Eva's face, mouth, tongue. Their eyes as focused and unblinking as hers.

The men did not notice Eva's eyes, but Alfred watched them for a time. They were distant and dispassionate. There was a look in them as if she saw how men reacted to her and hated them for it but continued to display herself in front of them regardless. The men, in their desire, were oblivious to how she looked at them.

After a time, wives and girlfriends grew uncomfortable with the display and tried to pull the men away. Dragging at hands and arms and coat tails. But the men wouldn't move at all, or did so reluctantly. Shifting towards the door with their heads still craned towards the stage.

The next day the tent was full.

"Found in a garden lush with fruit trees of all description, in the wildest corner of remote Mesopotamia, science can offer no explanation for Eva's remarkable proclivities. She has been subjected to every scientific experiment known to man, and every test modern medicine has been able to perfect, and yet no one, no matter how learned or skilled in the subtleties of science, has been able to ascertain precisely how or exactly why."

Alfred was standing near the bally with Hugo. The crowds had gone home, the men leaving reluctantly, walking Spanish towards the exit with their eyes still turned back on the sideshow tent.

"I hate the way she looks at me," Hugo said. He had one of his knives from the show and he was playing mumbledypeg with himself. Holding the knife, point down, against the top of his belt buckle and then letting it fall, digging blade first, into the dirt between his feet.

"Who?" Alfred asked.

"Her." Hugo let the knife fall from the middle of his chest. "That snake dame."

Alfred knew the look that she gave the audience as she reached her tongue out towards them. "Why does it bother you?"

Hugo shrugged. "Everything about her bothers me. She hardly ever talks to anybody. She doesn't eat with the rest of us."

Alfred shrugged. "The geek doesn't eat with us either," he said, trying to make a joke.

Hugo just shuddered. The knife was poised on the tip of his nose, his head tilted slightly forward. He let go and it tumbled quickly, slicing into the ground an inch from Hugo's unflinching left foot. "That's the least of it anyway. I dunno. There's something about her that rattles me. Normally, when a good lookin' dame gives me the eyeball... Don't laugh! It happens more than you think. There's lotsa tomatoes out there want to be with a guy like me. Dames in furs and jewels with chauffeurs comin' to pick me up. You think I'm kiddin' but you just wait. The things people do'll amaze you. Anyways, normally when a good lookin' dame gives me the eyeball I know just how to handle it. But this ain't like that." He placed the point of the knife on his forehead.

"What's it like?" Alfred thought he knew but he didn't want to admit it until someone else did first.

Hugo let the knife fall again. "Like nothin' I've ever felt before. I'm used to people starin' at me. It's happened all my life. But it never felt like this before. It's like she's sizin' you up for somethin'. Somethin' that she may want but that ain't likely to be any damn good for you." He bent and pulled the knife out of the ground, wiped the blade on his pant leg, and walked away towards his trailer.

∽

Alfred lit another cigarette and thought about what Hugo had said. It was her eyes that made Eva truly freakish, he realized - her eyes and what was behind them. Or what wasn't. Her mouth was just a distraction.

Alfred had walked to the end of the sideshow tent and turned towards the edge of the carnival grounds. He passed beyond the glow cast by the few electric lights that ringed the tents and the midway. A few yards further were woods that ran off far into the distance. Looking up,

Alfred could still make out the black outline of the treetops against the darkening sky. He stood for some time, looking at the stars that grew more and more numerous and distinct as the trees faded further from view. At some point he became aware of something moving through the trees in front of him. He was used to hearing noises in the darkness beyond the lights of the carnival. Rustlings and screechings and the snapping of twigs. They were so common that he usually ignored them. But this sound was different. It wasn't loud, but it was slow and close by, and moving along a path his ears could follow. It started somewhere off to his left and grew louder as it moved toward him, moved across in front of him in the darkness and then off to his right, gradually diminishing. It was something big - that much he knew - but there was no sound of footsteps.

He started walking to his right, following the sound. He moved quickly to close the distance and he could hear himself getting nearer. But just as he reached whatever was moving in the trees it sped up and raced ahead. He stopped and stared after it.

Alfred didn't bother following. He dropped the butt of his cigarette and pressed it into the ground. Then he rolled another one, lit it and tossed the match towards the dark woods, but it blew out before it went more than a foot.

"How long have you been in the sideshow game?" Alfred asked.

The carnival had set up just outside a small town in Southwestern Ontario. The kind of town that was good for a few days of modest crowds but where the scenery was beautiful. Alfred and Eva were walking by the river that wound past the town and skirted the fairgrounds.

"Not long at all. This is my first engagement." She stopped and stared down at the river.

This surprised Alfred. "Really?" he said. "I would have thought...I mean...with your..."

"I know what you mean. The way I am, you'd think I would have been on public display all my life. Well, no. They didn't do that. Mostly I was just hidden away. Sometimes I'd be shown to one person, or a small group. I presume that this was done in exchange for money, but nothing was ever said to me about it and I certainly never saw a penny. It felt to me, though, that most of the people who came in to see me were rich. So I suspect that whatever they charged was not inconsiderable. Twice a photographer came in and took a few pictures of me. But I never saw them and I don't know what became of them."

"When you say 'they', do you mean your parents?"

"It's rather complicated. Could I have a cigarette please?"

He rolled one for her. She bent her head forward, reached out and took it from him in a way that almost made Alfred recoil, but he held his hand there until she had taken the cigarette and placed it between her lips. Then he took a matchbook from his shirt pocket and struck one, holding it out towards her. She raised a hand and placed it over his to stop the match from shaking.

"Thank you," she said. "Let's see. How to explain this? As I was told it, my father wasn't around. He left long before I was born, so I have no idea who he was or what he looked like. And my mother may have wanted me at first, but that didn't last. She couldn't nurse me, or wouldn't. And they couldn't find anyone else to do it, not more than once anyway. So I was raised on goat's milk.

"We moved around a lot, although I was too young to remember. Then, when I was eight, she was offered money for me. We were living in this rooming house and the landlord offered her money. Or she went to them and offered to sell me. Either way, that's what happened. I don't expect my mother got a lot of money, but it wouldn't have taken much. And she wasn't very ambitious. By that point she didn't care. I think I frightened her."

She stopped and reached back over her shoulder and began rubbing and scratching. She opened her handbag and took out a small jar. It was clear glass with a white cream inside. She scooped some of the cream on to her fingers. "I have a skin condition," she said, rubbing vigorously. "A man at a medicine show said this would help."

"Does it?"

She smiled. "I don't think much helps," she said. "Anyway, I was with Uncle and Auntie for ten years. That's what they insisted I call them. Uncle and Auntie. They kept me locked in my room and I never saw anyone but them and the people they brought in to see me. And the photographer, twice. But they gave me things to read, books and magazines. I had a radio. And there was a window. It was screwed shut but I could see down into the alley behind the house. They fed me most days and he never hit me in the face. He knew better than that." She noted the look of concern on Alfred's face. "It wasn't so bad," she said. "He almost never used the buckle end."

"How did you get away?" Alfred asked, rubbing his temples.

"That's the strangest thing. One day they were just gone. The door to my room was locked but no one came in for a couple of days. At first, I thought it was just one of those times when they forgot to feed me, or chose not to. But it went on longer than it ever had before and I knew that they had left me. I managed to break the glass in the window and could just lean out far enough to reach a lamp post. I slid down that and went around to the front of the house. It was open but the house was practically empty. They'd either taken everything or they didn't have much to begin with.

"I had no idea how to take care of myself, but I knew I had to do something in order to eat. I knew about places like this and people like Gilroy. I'd read about that. So I started looking around and eventually I wound up here."

Alfred's upbringing had been normal and uneventful. Eva's he found to be highly disorienting. "Why did they leave you like that?" The first of the thousand questions he had that he could articulate.

"I think Auntie blamed me for the baby."

"I'm sorry?" Alfred said. "What baby?"

"Oh, she had a baby. Three years ago or so. For months and months I listened through the door. Sometimes it was hard because they were far away in the house and I couldn't hear very well but other times they were

14

right outside the door and I could listen to them cooing and laughing with the little girl. I could hear her gurgling and giggling. Sometimes I heard her crying. Then she started to walk and I heard her moving about on foot. Staggering at first and falling a lot. Then walking more and more solidly and steadily and falling less and less. Through the door, I listened to her learning to speak, getting taller, growing more and more curious. And then one day she disappeared.

"Auntie blamed me. But I was locked in my room. Where would I have put a three-year-old girl?"

"So what do you think happened?"

Eva drew deeply on the cigarette and shrugged. "All the time there were hoboes coming to the door, asking for food. There were pimps and dope fiends in the alley. Men always passing through, looking for work or something to steal. It could have been anyone," she said and turned back the way they had come.

∽

Everywhere they went, the show attracted tremendous publicity. Newspaper and magazine reporters clamoured for exclusive interviews. Photographers and their flashguns hunted in vain for candid photographs. In every church, the show was denounced from the pulpit. Large turnouts were guaranteed.

"Where did she come from? That is a tale unique in the annals of modern exploration. In the middle of the vast and trackless deserts of Mesopotamia a group of intrepid explorers, led by none other than the Great Gilroy himself, came upon an uncharted oasis. Lush and verdant and unknown to any of the nomadic peoples who make up this desolate and distant corner of the globe. But one old and wizened camel driver told of rumours of some remnant of the Garden of Eden. That is where Eva was found. Whence she was brought to civilization by camel caravan. She is offered here today in the interests of education and scientific learning. Is there a cure for her affliction? Is she the daughter of Eve? Was she sired by the Serpent? We leave that for you to decide."

∽

One evening, after all the men had been dragged away and the carnival closed, Gilroy sent Alfred to visit Eva.

"I'm getting worried about her, Alfred," Gilroy said. "She doesn't eat a god damn thing. I don't want her getting sick on us. You check on her and make sure she's okay. Get her any god damn thing she wants." Alfred had just turned for the door when Gilroy grabbed his elbow and turned him back. "Within reason, of course," he added.

"Yes, sir, Mr. Gilroy," Alfred said, trying not to smile. For days, he had been finding any excuse to stop by her trailer and talk to her. He would walk past several times a day in the hope of accidentally running into her. An official reason for being there seemed a kind of blessing.

∽

"I'm not very social," Eva said, the first time Alfred asked her to join him for dinner. "Growing up the way I did, I never really learned how to be around people. I prefer to eat alone." It had become routine now. Alfred would ask her to dinner, always couching the invitation in the form of Gilroy's growing concern. And the answer never varied. But Alfred still went to her trailer every evening.

"Dinner?"

"Thank you, Alfred, but no. I'm not hungry just now."

∽

"Alfred, have you seen Hugo?" Gilroy came walking down the midway, agitated. "I can't find the god damn half-pint anywhere and we're on in fifteen minutes."

Alfred shook his head. He couldn't remember seeing Hugo since the carnival closed the day before.

"Well, you're no god damn use," Gilroy said. "Ask around, will you? Check with the snake dame. And while you're there, remind her that we're on." And he moved on, stopping everyone he saw.

Alfred knocked on the door of Eva's trailer. "Come in, Alfred."

"How did you know it was me?"

"You're the only one who ever knocks on my door." She was in her costume and had a handkerchief wrapped around one hand.

"What happened to you?" Alfred asked. He reached out and gently took her wrist, turning her hand over. There was blood on the white cotton. "You've cut yourself."

"It's nothing. Just a scratch really." She removed the handkerchief and showed him. The bleeding had stopped but there was a ragged gash on her palm.

"What happened?"

"I was slicing peaches and the knife slipped."

Alfred nodded. "Gilroy needs you at the tent in five minutes. Oh, and apparently Hugo's missing. You haven't seen him have you?"

"Haven't you noticed? Hugo's always so careful to stay far away from me."

Alfred walked back to the bally to begin his day's work. All the way nagged by the thought that peaches weren't in season.

"Just one tenth of a dollar and you can behold all this and more. Tickets are on sale now. Please, no crowding. Everyone will get a chance to see this cavalcade of curiosities, this pageant of peculiarities. Tickets are on sale now in the doorway. Step right up and avoid the rush. Have your money ready."

Hugo never turned up. Although it seemed odd to Alfred that he would leave everything behind. All his clothes, a gramophone and a collection of jazz recordings, especially his knives. All except one.

Gilroy called the police but they weren't much interested in searching for a missing freak. Within the week Hugo had been replaced by another knife thrower. Not a midget but a man with one arm. "What's great about this," Gilroy said, "is that he's only got his right arm. And we tell everybody that he's left-handed. A left-handed knife thrower who doesn't have a left hand. What a god damn gimmick. You know how hard it is to throw a knife with your wrong god damn hand? Here, try it. Not at me, god damn it."

Within a month, nobody seemed to mention Hugo much at all.

∽

"I realize that you probably don't want to join me for dinner tonight," Alfred said.

"I'm sorry, Alfred. You must be getting tired of asking."

"Not really," he said with a shrug. "I reckon eventually you'll say yes." He pointed back over his shoulder towards the concession stands. "If not dinner, how about an ice cream? Mr. Gilroy thinks you're getting awfully thin."

"Please tell Mr. Gilroy not to worry so. I'm just fine. Some other time perhaps." They were at the door of her trailer now and he stood there, shuffling his feet. Being around her always made him feel nervous, a little unsettled. He started to offer her his hand to shake. But she reached out with both of hers, placed them on his shoulders and pulled him to her and kissed his cheek.

Then she kissed his ear and he felt her tongue for the first time. It reached down and touched his lobe, wiggling it back and forth, then traced the shape of the ear, and moved down to the point of his jaw and caressed the side of his neck.

She kissed him on the lips, and he felt her tongue moving into his mouth. Just a little at first, and then probing further and further. He started to gag but managed to suppress it as the tongue slithered into his throat and he felt more excitement than he had ever imagined. Then she pulled away from him.

"Good night, Alfred," she said.

He stood there for quite some time after she had gone inside. He felt a strong desire to knock on her door but didn't, hoping that if he willed it hard enough she would come back out to see him. That she would extend her hand and lead him inside. But nothing happened and eventually he left, walking slowly, looking back every few steps.

～

The next morning one of the Whitney midgets didn't show up for breakfast.

"It's Walter. Nobody's seen him since about six last evening," Gilroy said. "It doesn't matter to me. The god damn show's no worse without him. He couldn't sing worth a damn anyway."

"None of them can," Alfred pointed out. "Can't dance a lick either."

"I know, but he was the worst. The problem I got now is that his god damn wife's wailing and refuses to go on, and the little guy's vanished without a trace. She thinks he's run off with some dame from town or something. Just what I god damn need."

"No point talking to the cops?"

"Bah! As far as they're concerned we could all just disappear. They won't look for a singing midget anymore than they'd look for that knife tosser that we lost way back."

"Hugo," Alfred said.

"Yeah, I'm going to go," Gilroy said, rubbing his temples. "See if I can fix this god damn mess."

Walter never turned up. His wife, in the belief that she could find him and convince him to return to her, stayed behind too. Years later, Alfred imagined her still wandering around that town, asking people if they'd seen a really short man in spats and a fedora.

～

The carnival wound its way around Ontario, through Michigan and the Midwest and then back up into Manitoba. Everywhere they stopped, the audiences came. Although Alfred noticed no diminishing in size or excitement, as they returned to the country near the place where Eva first appeared, Gilroy decided that the show needed to be revitalized. To make it different so it would still be an event to those who had seen Eva before. Alfred knew that it didn't matter. He'd seen the way men looked at her repeated over and over again, in every town they passed through. He knew they would come back if there was no show at all. No carnival. No lights. No talk. Nothing but Eva.

"I've got a couple of really big ideas," Gilroy said. "Go talk to Eva and tell her I want to see her first thing tomorrow. I want to go over some plans with her to really spruce up this god damn show for the new season."

So, just as every other night, Alfred knocked at Eva's door. But this time there was no answer. He knocked again. Nothing. He called her name softly. Then more loudly. Still nothing. Finally, he tried the door handle. It turned and the door squeaked inward. Alfred looked inside but Eva was not where she usually sat, motionless on the cot. She wasn't at the small table at the other end of the trailer. And she was nowhere in between.

This was odd. He'd never known her not to be there. He went looking for her. Among the other trailers where perhaps she was out getting some air or chatting with the other attractions. But no. No one was out. He searched along the midway. Behind the Ten-In-One tent. He even walked down beyond the geek pit, although no one ever went around there much unless the carnival was open.

He had just turned back to go tell Gilroy he couldn't find her. He was hoping she hadn't taken off in the darkness and left the carnival behind - it wouldn't be the first time a freak had done that - when he saw her perhaps ten feet away. She was indistinct in the gloom, but the look of her was so embedded in his mind that just the vaguest outline was enough.

"Alfred," she said, "are you looking for me?" She came closer to him, and something about the way she moved held Alfred's eyes fast.

"Yes," he said, "but you weren't in your trailer."

"No, I wasn't." She moved closer still. "Have you come to offer me dinner?"

"No actually —"

"That's too bad," she said with a pout. "Because tonight I'm so hungry."

She kept sliding forward in her sinuous way until she was less than an arm's length from Alfred. He could feel her eyes on him. They were shining in the moonlight. Her breath was raspy and harsh. "Mr. Gilroy wants you," Alfred said.

"That may be. But I want you." Her arm stretched out and slipped around behind his back and he felt her nails press into him through his shirt. She pulled him close, and he remembered the excitement of kissing her, but something about the way she looked at him made him uneasy.

"Mr. Gilroy wants you," he repeated and tried to step back towards the heart of the carnival and Gilroy's trailer.

"But I want you. All of you," she said. She draped her other arm around him and kissed him deeply. Against his better judgment, he responded. Then she drew her face away. "I want you inside me," she said, and slipped around to his side.

Alfred had run into all kinds of women in his time with the carnival. But he'd never been propositioned so bluntly before. "I want you inside me." Her mouth was pressed tight against his ear, both her arms wrapped around him, pinning his arms to his sides. He felt one of her legs moving across his shins. Her tongue probed his ear in a now familiar way.

Alfred could not remember ever being held so tightly. He felt her other leg rubbing across the backs of his knees. Her arms squeezed him steadily. Her tongue traced around the edge of his ear and her breath hissed. She nibbled his earlobe and then he felt her lips touch the top of his ear and the bottom at the same time.

"I want you inside me," she said again, this time distorted, the way you talk to your dentist. Her tongue still played on the side of his face, tasting him, and he realized he was having trouble breathing.

At first, he thought it was just the shortness of breath he sometimes felt when he was aroused. But then he realized it was accompanied by a growing pain in his chest and a numbness spreading down his legs. He bent his head forward and saw that both her legs were now twisted around him, coiled like six feet of rope. And her arms constricted his chest tightly and more tightly.

His ribs and the bones in his thighs felt like they would snap any instant. He was sure he heard them creaking under the strain.

"God damn," he thought. The squeezing got tighter. He thought of Hugo and the missing Whitney midget. It had been weeks since the last disappearance. *I'm so hungry,* she had said.

He was desperate to run, but could do little more than wiggle his toes. He tried to cry out, but there seemed to be not enough breath in his lungs. He felt tears of frustration. Then he realized there was still one thing he could do, one last desperate way to help himself. He tensed all his muscles and pitched himself sideways. At first, he was afraid it wouldn't work. Then, mercifully, they started to topple. Slowly at first and then more quickly, Alfred bracing himself for impact with the ground. But it never came. Instead Alfred suddenly felt canvas against his face. Canvas that gave and then sprang back pushing them the other way. At first, Alfred had no idea what it was. Then, as the two of them rolled down the canvas wall, it came to him. The geek pit. He heard movement inside the enclosure and he wished he had the capacity to call for help. But her pressure on him was relentless and smothering. Besides, he knew that, even if he could scream at the top of his lungs, it wouldn't matter. The geek would probably be drunk and useless anyway.

They hit the ground. Eva squeezing tighter now, lying on top of him, the pressure causing her sinewy arms and legs to dig into his body. He could barely breathe. His vision blurred. Even she, so close to him and crushing him inexorably, was hard to see. Then, just as he was sure he would pass out, the pressure stopped and he was free.

∽

When he came back into Gilroy's trailer, Alfred felt a little dizzy and off-kilter. The way he imagined you might feel with a minor inner ear infection. It distorted your balance and made the world look slightly askew - in a way that made you feel you'd never be able to look at things the same way again.

"You look like hell," Gilroy said. "Where's Eva?"

"She's dead."

"What?" Gilroy's feet dropped from his desktop to the floor.

"The geek got her."

"What do you mean, the geek got her?"

"That's what I mean. The geek got her. He bit her head clean off. Well, not clean. But off."

"What?"

Alfred nodded. He was staring straight ahead, not looking at Gilroy or Laszlo. Just picturing it over and over. Himself almost crushed by the suffocating grip of Eva. Lying on the ground, feebly trying to squirm away but held fast. And then suddenly the pressure grew less and then less again and he brought his eyes around to see why, and there was the geek, dragging her from him. Her mouth was open wide and she hissed and spat at the geek but he didn't seem to notice. Alfred thought this was all some kind of dream. The vision he'd carry with him into whatever world came next. But, as the pressure on his body eased, the mist over his eyes cleared and he saw that it was not a dream at all.

"Yeah, the geek got her," he said. "He grabbed her by the shoulders. Then he opened his mouth until it was about this wide." He held up his hands a foot and a half apart. "And then he popped it over her head - all the way down to her shoulders, practically. She was screaming but it got all muffled once her head was right inside his mouth and then he chomped down."

In forty years in show business, Gilroy had seen a lot of things and heard a bunch more. But this was something new. "What happened to the head?"

"I just told you. The geek bit it off."

"No, no, no. Did he swallow it or spit it out?"

"Oh, I don't know. I don't remember that part."

"Well, we'll find out soon enough." He turned to Laszlo, holding his hands a good foot further apart than Alfred had held his. "He opened his god damn mouth this wide. Did you know he could do that?"

Laszlo shook his head. "Nope. Never done anything like that. Least ways not so's anybody seen it. Biggest thing he ever bit the head off before was that wild turkey a year or two back when we done that special Thanksgiving show."

"Oh yeah," Gilroy said. "What a god damn adventure that was." He turned back to Alfred. "How did he seem?"

"Who?"

"The geek. The god damn geek. After he bit her head off, how did he seem?"

Alfred shrugged. "I dunno. I looked back after my head cleared a bit and he was just sitting there leaning against the side of the pit. Looking pretty happy, I guess. Pleased with himself."

"He didn't look any the worse for wear?"

Alfred shook his head. "No, he looked fine. And she was lying there on the ground with her head gone."

"He got the whole thing?"

"Who?"

"The geek, god damn it. The god damn geek. He got her whole head? Not just part of it?"

"It sure looked like he got the whole thing to me. But like I said, I don't remember too much after he bit down." Alfred picked up the bottle of whiskey on Gilroy's desk and didn't bother about a glass. As he tilted the bottle to drink, he was interested to notice that his hand was quite steady. He felt like he'd learned something really important about life and, if he was patient, eventually the nature of the lesson would become plain to him.

"He got the whole god damn thing, eh?" Gilroy said half to himself. "Good. That's good."

"How can that be good?" Laszlo asked. "We just lost our star attraction. What can be good about that?"

"What do you mean 'lost' our star? We just found one. A god damn great big star."

"What do you mean?"

"I mean the god damn geek."

Laszlo looked puzzled but Alfred understood. Even as he was walking over to Gilroy's trailer, leaving the geek sitting on the ground with Eva's headless body in his lap, Alfred understood the possibilities.

He knew how Gilroy would react. In that moment, he also knew that he had what it took to make it as a showman.

Laszlo said, "We can't have a geek biting people's heads off as part of the show. We have enough trouble with the cops when it's rats and chickens."

Gilroy stared at Laszlo. "What are you talking about, human heads? Nobody's going to be biting off anybody's god damn head." He turned to Alfred. "Would you say a human head is about the same size as a bowling ball?"

"A what?"

"A bowling ball. A bowling ball. Would you say that a human head is about the same size as a god damn ten-pin bowling ball?"

Laszlo shrugged and Alfred said, "I guess so."

"You used to bowl, Laszlo. Do you still have that bowling ball?"

"Yeah," Laszlo said.

"Well don't just stand there. Get the god damn thing."

Laszlo left the trailer and came back five minutes later with the ball. "Let me see that." Gilroy took it from him, hefted it, inspected it from all angles. "All right," he said. "Let's go see how this god damn idea works." He left the trailer, cradling the bowling ball. Laszlo went after him. And Alfred toasted the future and had another drink.

Murdoch's Wife

How much does it cost to have somebody killed?" Murdoch asked.

"How long is a piece of string?" Kieran replied.

"What the hell does that mean?"

"It means," Kieran said, "that it depends."

"Depends on what?"

"Depends on who it is. You want me to whack the guy runs the bar down your street, it'll cost you X. You want me to whack the Prime Minister or the captain of the Leafs, that's something else entirely and it'll cost you Y. And I really don't like having to kill women. So if you want me to whack a chick, I either won't do it or I'll do it but I wouldn't feel right taking money for it. So who do you want me to cap?"

"I want you to kill whoever's fucking my wife. How much is that going to cost me?"

"Were you not listening, my friend? That depends entirely on whether your wife is getting her ass bounced by the guy who runs the bar down the street or the captain of the Leafs or the Prime Minister or another chick. So who is it?"

"How the hell should I know? You think she gives me names?"

"Ah. Well, that creates some difficulty. You see, I'm a craftsman, not a clairvoyant."

"Yeah, well that's the other part of the job. I want to hire you to find out who the bastard is before you whack him. I don't care how you do it. I just want him dead."

"But you need me to find out who this person is first."

"Yeah."

Kieran sipped some beer and thought for a minute. "That'll cost you extra," he said. "I'm a craftsman, not a private detective."

"Charge me X plus Z, I don't care. I want him found and I want him popped. And there's one more thing I want."

"And what might that be?"

"I want you to bring me the guy's fucking head."

"That," Kieran said, "will definitely cost extra."

Murdoch raised his hands in front of him, fingers splayed, in an expression of mock surprise. "What a shock," he said. "And since we're on the topic of dough, there's one other thing. Now, it's not that I'm of a suspicious or untrusting nature. I'm not. But there's nothing to say that you couldn't go out, pick any poor dumb prick off the street and whack him and cut off his head and bring it to me and tell me it was the guy."

Kieran thought about the chances that he might do this and decided they were slim at best. "I'm a craftsman," he said, "not a psychopath."

"Yeah, well that's as may be, but I'll still need proof that the guy whose head you bring me is the same guy's been getting head from my wife."

"I'm assuming you mean a videotape or photographs or something."

"Yeah, or signed affidavits from a bunch of witnesses, which seems less likely to me. How much do you reckon all that'll cost me?"

Kieran smiled. "How long," he asked, "is a very long piece of string?"

Two hours later, Kieran said to Murdoch's wife, "Your husband wants me dead." They were lying in bed in the loft of the two-storey North Toronto apartment that Kieran had rented under another name so that he'd have a quiet and private place to spend afternoons with Murdoch's wife.

"How do you know this?"

"He hired me to find the guy you're screwing and kill him."

"So he hired you to kill yourself, basically. Oh, brother. What are you going to do?"

"I'm going to think on it," Kieran said. "Now turn around."

For a professional killer, Kieran kept his life as ordinary as possible. He shopped at the local markets and he said hello to his neighbours. He paid his parking tickets on time and he made regular donations to a variety of charities. He kept normal hours, waking every morning at seven, and he never played his stereo too loudly. The last thing he wanted was to stick out by seeming mysterious, peculiar or unusually aloof. When anyone asked what he did, Kieran told them he was in marketing, self-employed, specializing in strategic and concept development and execution. He figured that was at least partly true.

Then one day a neighbour said that the board of the telephone crisis line he was on was looking for a marketing person. They were already hip-deep in accountants and lawyers but someone like Kieran, with a marketing background, could be really helpful in fund-raising and helping recruit phone volunteers. Kieran thought about it for a day or two. He realized that, much as he had no problem with people having their lives ended abruptly by others, he did see the need for those considering self-destruction to have somewhere to turn. So he accepted. Kieran liked to think that, for a killer, he had a very highly developed social conscience.

It turned out that Murdoch's wife also sat on the board. And when she walked into the room during Kieran's first meeting and he saw her for the first time, his stomach twisted in an unfamiliar way. And every time he saw her after that, the reaction was the same.

Over the course of several board meetings, Kieran and Murdoch's wife talked and were increasingly drawn to one another. Soon they were having lunch together. And, although she told him emphatically that she was not unhappy in her marriage, they were in bed together within a matter of weeks.

"I've thought about it," Kieran said to Murdoch's wife two days later. It was Friday afternoon and the sun was very bright through the skylight above Kieran's bed. "There's only one solution."

"And I'm guessing it isn't suicide."

"I'm really not the type," Kieran said.

"I can see that," she said.

Kieran looked at her with a smile. "No, the answer is you'll just have to sleep with somebody else. We'll film it or something. And then I'll kill him. Your husband will be happy. I'll get paid, so I'll be happy. And we can carry on as usual. So you'll be happy."

"So everybody's happy."

"Yeah. Except the dead guy. He won't be too thrilled, I don't expect. But at least he won't notice for long."

"The only thing I'm a little unhappy about is that you basically want me to sleep with someone I don't know."

"Only once. And it doesn't have to be someone you don't know." He reached up and pushed the dark hair out of her eyes. "I'm sure lots of guys you know would jump at the chance."

Kieran was not sure if he had ever been in love. But weeks before he first took Murdoch's wife to bed, he felt himself falling in love with her. Whenever he entered a board meeting his eyes sought her out. He had never been one to wait for a phone call before, but he felt small pangs of anticipation build in him when he thought she might call and equal measures of disappointment when the phone rang and it was not her.

When he considered it logically, he was not sure why he felt the way he did about her. She gave no indication that she would leave her husband. She frequently promised to do things that remained undone or cancelled plans he was looking forward to with excuses that Kieran knew were not true.

She had cancelled out on theatre tickets, on summer weekends at cottages north of the city and winter weekends at country inns. It was obvious to him that her emotional commitment was less than complete. Still, he wanted her. And as he waited, he watched her behaviour and his own with growing irritation. And he played by her rules.

30

"I know who you can kill," Murdoch's wife said.

"Who might that be?"

"He's a doctor. His name's Lackman."

"Why him?"

She turned over on her stomach. "Rub my back," she said. As he did so, she explained, "I went to see him a few times about this little problem I was having a year ago or so, and he lives near my house, and we've run into each other on the street a few times, and he's always really friendly. Anyway, at some point, my husband became convinced that we were having an affair. Mmm, down a little. There. That's good. He actually has come on to me a couple of times. It was pretty subtle, but I know he'd like to have a fling. He stands too close to me and he touches me a lot. Getting him into bed shouldn't be any problem. Anyway, he's not totally hideous. And he's already a suspect in my husband's mind, so that will help when you bring in his head."

"And you never slept with this guy?"

"Don't be ridiculous," she said.

Murdoch's wife had been sleeping with Doctor Lackman for about seven months. She did it some Tuesday mornings and most Thursdays over the lunch hour. Days when she was not seeing Kieran.

"I want you to do something for me," she said to the doctor as they lay beneath the ceiling fan.

His eyes were closed but his mind was racing. "Anything."

She traced irregular shapes on his chest with her fingernail and said, "I want you to kill someone."

"What?" His eyes popped open and he turned and propped himself up on an elbow.

"I want you to kill someone," she repeated. "And then cut off his head."

"What?" He stared at her, thinking he must have misheard.

"You're a doctor," she said. "You know about this. You can cut off his head. I've heard about these anatomy classes medical students all take, where you cut up derelicts and people who sign that form on their driver's licence. This will be no different."

"What?" he said again. "No different? You're asking me to kill a man and cut off his head. That's substantially different in my book."

"Why? In school, didn't you cut off someone's head?"

"Yes, but..."

"And I know you've killed a couple of people."

His face turned a shade redder. "I didn't kill anyone. Those people just died, and it was during surgery. Nobody could prove I did anything wrong."

"Yes, but you know in your heart things might have gone better if you'd been a little less hung over."

"Why?" he asked. "Where did this come from? One minute I'm lying here all relaxed and the next minute you're talking about murder."

"Here's where it came from. My husband thinks I'm having an affair," she said. "And he's going to hire someone to kill my lover. That, my darling, is you. Now, my husband tends to do the things he says he'll do, so I believe him. And I'd hate to see anything happen to you if it could be avoided. So I need you to kill someone, in order to save your own skin."

Lackman thought about this for a minute. Murdoch's wife could almost feel the wheels grinding round. "So you want me to kill the guy who's been hired to kill me."

Murdoch's wife laughed. "Oh, brother," she said. "That would be the worst thing you could do. Because the guy who's been hired to kill you has to report back to my husband with your head in a box or a bag or something. No. If you kill him, my husband will know something went wrong and he'll just hire somebody else. No. We have to make a deal with the killer to take my husband's money and leave you alone. Then we find somebody else, I take him to bed and you kill him." She smiled at him sweetly. "Then you give the head to the killer and he takes it away. My husband's happy. The killer's doubly happy since he got paid and didn't actually have to kill anybody. And we can carry on just like always."

"Why don't we just pay the killer again to kill someone other than me?"

"We could do that, but it's very expensive." And she told him how much Kieran was going to charge her husband for the job. She inflated the price considerably, sensing that Lackman would not know how to begin to check. And also knowing he was tight with a dollar, and wanting to discover how much he was willing to do for her.

Lackman responded true to form. "So I have to kill a complete stranger."

"No necessarily. There must be a colleague or two that you'd like to see dead. Or I could find someone."

"Yes, I think that's a good idea. But isn't this plan awfully complicated?"

"You're a doctor," she said. "I'm sure you can figure it out."

Then she reached out towards him and Lackman felt the breath thickening in his throat and knew he would do exactly as she wanted.

"Oh," she murmured, "there's one other thing. Do you own a video camera?"

Kieran was sitting at his usual table at the back of the bar when Murdoch walked in. The room was large and virtually deserted. "Good afternoon." Kieran smiled and waved a hand at the opposite chair.

Murdoch said, "How much?" as he sat down.

Kieran told him.

"What?" Murdoch said very loudly.

"Please be more discreet," Kieran said, "or I'll have to ask you to look for another supplier."

Murdoch leaned forward across the table and continued in a stage whisper. "That's an incredible amount of money."

"What you're asking me to do is an incredible thing. You want me to videotape a man having sex with your wife, then kill him, which means doing it in front of a witness, then cut off his head, then transport it across town like a candied ham. And after it's over I presume you don't want to get arrested for it. And I know I don't. That takes an extreme amount of caution, preparation and attention to detail. And also an extreme amount of money. And it's all up front. Take it or leave it."

"Can I give you a cheque?"

"Sure," Kieran said.

Murdoch's expression told Kieran that he had meant the question as a joke. "I'll just invoice your company," Kieran explained. "That way you can write it off." He'd done this before and it didn't bother him at all. He considered it a good idea to have a record of revenue and regular tax payments.

"Yeah, right. And what do you invoice me for?"

"Consulting on strategies to eliminate a competitive threat," Kieran said.

Murdoch thought about this for a moment. "Okay," he said. "Back-date the invoice a month and I'll pay you right away."

"I'll send a courier tomorrow," Kieran said.

Murdoch's wife was in a state of some confusion. Ever since Kieran told her what he did for a living, she had felt some unease. Given her background as a social worker, it made her frequently uncomfortable to be so close to a man who earned a handsome living by killing other people. Her friends, who did not know about Kieran at all, told her she had changed. She felt she had lost some of the focus in her life. And she felt a gentle pressure from him. It was obvious he wanted more than twice weekly trysts but, much as she had told him she had longed for someone like him, she really didn't want anything to change. There was a large part of her that felt it was time to say goodbye to Kieran. She had already begun detaching herself.

Lackman was a different matter. He wanted nothing but sex. He was too self-centred and shallow to offer anything more. The only disappointment for Murdoch's wife was that, unlike Kieran, the doctor was a pedestrian and mediocre lover and, despite considerable practice, he didn't seem to improve. But he was not frightening to her in the way that Kieran was. And she got the sense that ending a relationship with Kieran needed to be done on a permanent basis. He felt much too dangerous to leave alive. Unfortunately, permanence was not a strong suit of hers. She was counting on Lackman to help her out.

Sometimes she thought she should just dump them both and work it out with her husband.

Kieran made an appointment to see Doctor Lackman. He fabricated symptoms and, on the scheduled day, went and sat in Lackman's waiting room for half an hour, pretending to read an old *Toronto Life* while surveying the room and the other patients as they came and went. Kieran was successful because he was thorough. He never killed anyone without first getting to know them. Their habits and their patterns. Unlike others in his profession, he was not averse to meeting with future victims on some pretence or other. And he was quite curious about the doctor.

Finally, Kieran was called into an examining room where Lackman measured everything that could be measured and explored every place that could be explored. "You're healthy as anything," he said. "You must take really good care of yourself."

Kieran looked Lackman right in the eye and said, "I plan to live for a long time."

Kieran followed Lackman closely for several days, becoming fully acquainted with the doctor and his comings and goings. Then, on the next Friday, he said to Murdoch's wife, "Start getting your man primed."

"When are you going to do it?" She felt a shiver of excitement.

"Next week. We'll sort that out in a minute."

"How are you going to do it?"

Kieran shrugged. "I'll work that out. Don't worry, you won't get any blood on you. But we have to do it some place anonymous. I want you to bring him here."

"Here?"

"Yeah. Bring him here."

"How do I do that?"

"Tell him it's an apartment you borrowed from a friend. I don't know. You'll think of something. Just get him here and I'll take care of everything else."

Murdoch's wife suggested the following Thursday at noon, and Kieran agreed.

In the apartment that Kieran rented under another name, there was an electrical outlet in the wall at the head of the bed just above the top of the mattress. The first time they'd used the apartment, Murdoch's wife had touched the outlet and said, "Isn't that dangerous?"

Kieran shook his head. "Only if you stick a fork in it. Even then, I guess not. Power's controlled by that switch." He pointed to the switch on the wall next to the door of the room. "I thought your husband was an electrician or something. You oughta know something about it."

"Why? That's what *he* does. We don't talk about it much."

On Thursday morning, Kieran opened the breaker panel in the apartment and threw switches until he found he right one. Then he went upstairs to the bedroom and pulled the bed away from the wall. With a small screwdriver he undid the plate covering the outlet and went to work. When he was finished, he pushed the bed back into place. Then, one corner at a time, he raised the legs of the bed and placed round rubber feet under them. He readjusted the carpet on the hardwood beside the bed, then took out four tacks and a small hammer and fixed the mat to the floor. Then he went downstairs, turned the power back on and went out to have a coffee.

From his seat in the window of the café across the street, Kieran watched Murdoch's wife arrive at the front door of the building. She let herself in and disappeared behind the glass and up the stairs. Ten minutes later, Kieran watched Dr. Lackman arrive. The doctor buzzed, the door opened and he too vanished inside.

When they were together the day before, Kieran told Murdoch's wife that a friend who knew about these things had set up a hidden video camera that would go on automatically. Then Kieran would give Lackman and Murdoch's wife time for a good, healthy romp before he let himself into the apartment and subjected the good doctor to an extreme case of *coitus interruptus*.

He looked at his watch and signalled the waitress for a refill.

In the apartment, Lackman was clearly agitated as Murdoch's wife pressed into his hands the pistol belonging to her husband that she had taken from the house. "I'm not sure about this," he said. "Look at my hands." They were shaking considerably.

"Don't worry. He'll be naked and lying down and focused on me. You can do it. Just stay in the closet until I get up to go to the bathroom. He'll watch me walk there. He always does. That's when you come out and shoot him."

Lackman gave her the same look of comprehension you see on the face of a dog that's just been told how to mix cocktails.

When his coffee was finished, and he felt he had given the happy couple enough time, Kieran reached into his pocket and left several large coins on the table. Then he walked slowly to the corner and crossed the street with the light. Taking out his key he let himself into the building, whistling softly. He climbed the stairs with one hand lightly on the banister. When he let himself into the apartment all he could hear was Dexter Gordon playing *I'm a Fool to Want You.*

He went up the stairs to the bedroom on the second floor and stood in the doorway, with one hand resting on the doorjamb.

"Where is he?" Kieran asked Murdoch's wife, who was alone in the bed.

"He cancelled on me," she said without missing a beat. "Come here."

Doctor Lackman didn't like being in the closet. He'd never liked enclosed spaces and he found that being cooped up, coupled with the prospect of killing another man, was causing him to tense up. Breathing slowly and deeply, he tried to fill his mind with happier thoughts. From somewhere he could smell the musk of her perfume. He realized the closet held clothes of silk and cotton, all she ever wore. He imagined her standing before him, the fabric slipping off her body. The he started to wonder what her perfume was doing on clothing in a stranger's closet.

He was distracted by the sound of his victim entering the room. He heard footsteps and a few words exchanged but they were muffled and indistinct. His hands began sweating and he switched the gun from one to the other, alternately wiping his palms on a crisp white blouse.

He leaned forward to try and hear what was being said more clearly. The panic was building in him. It must have been long enough. He wasn't looking forward to shooting an unarmed man in the back, but it was rapidly becoming preferable to spending any more time entombed in someone else's closet. It was time to get out.

"Come on," Murdoch's wife said again. "Come to bed."

At that moment, the doors of the walk-in closet slapped open and Lackman stepped out. He was wearing boxer shorts and he looked slight and insignificant despite the pistol clenched in his delicate hands. From the bed, Murdoch's wife groaned, "Not yet."

"I'm going to kill you," Lackman said, voice wavering. Then he paused and peered at Kieran more closely, "Wait a minute, I know you."

Since he didn't pull the trigger right away, and was obviously going through the Rolodex in his head to figure out why he recognized Kieran's face, it was obvious that the doctor was not a true killer. So Kieran took the time to look at Murdoch's wife, lying on the bed, half covered by the tangled flannel sheets. "I really wanted to be with you," he said. "Before he shoots me, get out of bed so I can have one last good look at you."

Murdoch's wife hesitated for a moment but then she began to get out of bed. She rose as she always did. Languorously, dropping her slender legs over the edge of the bed. Then placing a hand on the head of the metal bed frame and setting her feet squarely on Kieran's mat. As her feet touched down, Kieran reached up and threw the switch on the wall. Instantly, the current streaked along the wires to the outlet at the head of the bed, then raced along the copper wire Kieran had installed that led from the hot wire in the outlet to the metal bed frame. The current surged through the frame into the sleek and beautiful body of Murdoch's wife and through her body into the metal plate Kieran had placed beneath the worn carpet at the side of the bed on which her small, soft feet rested.

Lackman had never seen a person being electrocuted before and he did as Kieran thought he would. He lowered the gun and turned to watch the bed and the spasms of its occupant. Kieran took his own pistol out and shot the doctor through the head. Then, after giving Murdoch's wife a few extra seconds of juice, he switched the current off. He had never seen anyone electrocuted either and he found it quite educational.

He knew it would take the cops about a minute and a half to make a connection between the electrocuted woman and the dead doctor and the electrician husband turned cuckold. By then, Kieran would be back home, talking to neighbours and shaking his head along with the rest of the board. He could imagine, too, the reactions of her friends. Murdoch's wife hideously murdered in a secret love nest. Who would ever have imagined such a tawdry thing of her?

He left the doctor's head where it was. There was no need anymore. He took one last look at the crumpled woman smouldering on the floor. Then he went downstairs, locking the door behind him. It was too bad about Murdoch's wife. Oh well. At least the cheque had cleared.

Boogie Man

Ki ing pulled his car to a stop in front of Diamond's house just as the ambulance drove away. He watched it ease onto the street and drive half a block before switching on its headlights, the siren and the flashing light on its roof remaining silent and dim. Climbing out of his car, King walked to the front door. Two men stopped him there, but they weren't cops so King knew Gore hadn't told anybody yet.

"Yeah?" one of the men said. Both stood with their backs to the big double doors and their arms folded across their chests.

"King. Gore sent for me."

"Yeah." One of them stepped back and let King in through the door, closing it again immediately.

King stood in the hallway on the deep pile carpet and looked around. He had never liked Diamond's house. It was ornate and expensively furnished, but somehow seemed austere. Busy, but empty.

King looked at the paintings in their heavy gilt frames lining the walls along the hall and up the big circular staircase where they vanished in the darkness of the second floor.

"King." Gore appeared in the doorway off to the left. Small, round, untidy and rumpled, he looked like a janitor. He appeared to have slept in his suit, but King knew he had been up all night. His call, an hour earlier, had woken King up.

King followed Gore into the room. It was Diamond's trophy room, filled with awards, gold records and photographs, all of Diamond with one celebrity or another, or accepting some honour.

There was another man in the room, sitting cross-legged on the couch, his arms loosely folded, resting in his lap. He smiled at King, but his eyes remained still.

"This is an old friend of mine," Gore said. "John Devereaux. He's a doctor."

Devereaux rose with a smooth uncoiling of limbs. He held out a slender hand. "Hello," he said softly, the word rolling off his tongue like syrup.

King shook hands and nodded. "Doctor, eh? What kind?"

Devereaux smiled without revealing any teeth. "Let's just say I'm in private practice."

Gore chuckled and settled into a big wing chair by the fire. It was early October, but cold. The doctor sank back to the couch. King hesitated, then took a chair opposite Gore.

"When did he die?" King asked, sticking his feet towards the fire and looking at Devereaux.

The doctor shrugged. "Probably around one or two, but the exact time doesn't really matter."

"It does to me. I'm the one who has to feed it to the press."

Gore prodded a big log on the fire with a poker and sent up a shower of sparks.

"How did it happen?" King asked.

"Heart attack, possibly. Perhaps induced by alcohol. Or drugs. Or both. I'd really need an autopsy to discern exactly."

"Was he alone?"

"Oddly, yes. As far as we know."

"What about cops? They're gonna want a full investigation."

Gore still poked and jabbed at the fire. "Leave that to me," he said. He seemed very calm. King had felt sure he would be either in a rage or sick with anxiety.

King himself was not too upset, but then he never cared much for Diamond. He found Diamond abusive and arrogant and not nearly talented enough to deserve all the attention he received. But King knew he was partly to blame for Diamond's success. He was responsible for hype, promotion, and building anything connected with Johnny Diamond up to a major international event.

Even so, King didn't have the same vested interest in Diamond that Gore had. King did most of the flack, but Gore ran the show. Without Diamond, King was out of a product to plug, but Gore was out of a burgeoning corporation to run. He seemed too calm for a man who stood to lose a multi-million dollar investment. No one could expect the manager and mentor of one of the top pop idols of his age to be so cool when his star died just one week before he was due to begin a ninety-date tour.

King watched Gore as the shadow and firelight alternated on his face, and waited to hear more. "I don't think they'll bother us much," was all Gore said.

King didn't agree or disagree. "What about the tour?"

"What about it?"

"Now that it's off, what are the losses going to look like?"

Gore set the poker back in the cast-iron stand next to the fireplace and settled back in his chair, his fingers steepled under his chin. "There won't be any losses."

"What? How can there be no losses?"

"It's very simple, King. We are not cancelling the tour."

"What?" King looked at him blankly.

"You heard. We open Friday as scheduled."

King knew then why Gore had been so calm and quiet. He had lost his mind. "And just what the hell do you expect to do? Sell out ninety shows with nothing on stage but the microphones?"

Gore shook his head. "We won't need microphones at all."

"Huh?"

Gore smiled. "King," he said, "this was going to be a big tour for Diamond. We think he should try to make it."

"What are you talking about? The man is dead, Gore. Dead."

"Exactly."

Gore and Devereaux watched King with sated looks. The germ of an idea started to grow in King's mind, but he forced it down.

Gore brought it back up. "Remember, King, when Elvis died? Remember the thousands of fans who lined up for hours outside Graceland in the hope of God knows what? They were all over the place. They needed guards to keep them away. At the funeral. At his grave. Don't you think if each of them was charged five bucks to file through the house and look at the body they would have done it?"

He was speaking very softly, almost in a whisper, leaning forward across the front of the fire towards King. "Sure, there would've been a few who'd refuse. A few who'd be too noble. And there'd be some who'd only go in for free. But most of them would have gone. At five bucks a head. Multiply that by the number of fans Elvis had and you're talking about a hell of a lot of money. How many fans does Diamond have? We won't make a cent less than we would if Diamond hadn't kicked."

King looked from Gore to Devereaux.

Gore laughed. "When the curtain goes up on Friday night, Diamond will be on stage. Christ, we could put an urn full of his ashes in the spotlight and they'd still pay to see it. Imagine what they'd pay to run their hands through those ashes in the hope that one or two flakes would stick to their sweaty palms." His eyes were wide, reflecting the firelight. He spoke with hushed intensity. "The possibilities are limitless."

"They won't all come up here just to see a corpse," King said, still half convinced that Gore was joking.

Gore was out of his chair. "Of course not. That's why the tour is on. When we're finished here, we just close the lid, nail it down, and move somewhere else. People don't just want to see him here, they want to see him everywhere. Every city in this country and half the cities in the world are crawling with Flawless Johnny Diamond fans. There's a market for the guy dead or alive and why the hell should we let it slip through our fingers when we can get him anywhere in the world for the cost of excess baggage and no bitching about the accommodations? No food complaints, no drug busts, no torn-up hotels or smashed equipment. It'll be like going on tour with Marie Osmond." He brought his knuckles to his mouth and gnawed. King wasn't sure if the action was brought on by the thought of low overhead or Marie Osmond. He hoped it was low overhead. "This is a dream." Gore flung his hands wide. "This is the greatest angle in history, and I'm giving you the chance to promote it."

"Diamond's dead, Gore," King said again, not sure he wanted to promote anything like it. "In a few days he's going to start to rot, and he'll stink like hell. And I guarantee nobody's going to pay to sit in a concert hall all night just so they can smell some guy decomposing."

Gore chuckled. "That won't happen."

"How are you going to stop it?"

"We'll freeze him." His eyes were wild and his chuckle turned to maniacal laughter directed at the ceiling and ringing through the dark room.

King turned to the doctor. "Will that work?"

Devereaux nodded. "It should. It should keep him fresh long enough to serve our purposes."

"Our purposes?"

"Diamond is a star. Even dead, he's going to need a lot of care. The best care."

"The kind of care you can provide?"

Devereaux inclined his head modestly.

"Gentlemen, shall we drink to the future success of the late Johnny Diamond?" Gore asked, crossing to a mahogany liquor cabinet by the far wall and raising a cut-glass decanter of Scotch. Twelve years old if it was a day. He poured out three stiff drinks. It tasted like money.

"Where's the body now?" King asked with the Scotch sitting warm and golden in his stomach, almost masking the uneasy feeling he felt growing there.

"Safe," Gore said. "We're keeping a very close eye on him until Friday. And then we're going to rock the rock world."

"At least no one will be able to say he died in New Haven," King said.

Gore laughed and drained his glass. He smashed it in the fireplace.

Devereaux and Gore had done a lot of planning in the two hours between the discovery of Diamond's body and Gore's abrupt call to

King.

"He's being taken care of right now," Devereaux said, his gaunt face slightly flushed from the Scotch and the heat of the fire. "We're storing him in a full-length freezer for a day or two. We have somebody working on a special casket for him, with satin lining and mahogany panelling. It's just a fancy freezer really, but then this is a pretty fancy side of beef. That will be his new home." Devereaux smiled. "He'll never get a chance to thaw out."

Gore did a few steps of a jig in front of the fire. "I told you, King, it's perfect. It's an opportunity too good to pass up."

King was still not sure. He pursed his lips and thought about it. "What happens if it bombs?"

"It won't," Gore said. "And if it does, what the hell? Diamond's kicked anyway, so we've got nothing else to lose. And when we win, we win in a very big way. We're going a long way fast with this thing. I want you along for that ride."

"You, me and Devereaux?"

"That's right," Gore said with a toothy smile. "Right now, the doctor and I have a few more things to take care of. I'll call you when everything's set to go. I'm glad you're with us, King." He ushered King to the front door, leaving the doctor sipping Scotch and smiling.

King left the house uncertain whether he was glad to be with them or not.

ꙅ

The lineup was already over a block long, curving around the corner and out of sight, when King got to the concert hall. The doors weren't slated to open for two hours. Gore had been right. Only a few of the people holding tickets had redeemed them. Others kept them for use at this new exhibit, and an almost infinite supply was available at the door.

From the looks of things, Gore would have no trouble making up for the few returned tickets. King watched the string of people, ranging from their teens to late middle age, shivering in the fall drizzle. After a moment, he turned down an alley next to the theatre and knocked on a side fire door.

An usher opened the door. "King?" he asked.

"Yes."

The usher stepped back to let King inside. The first thing he noticed was the chill. He shivered involuntarily at finding so little relief from the dampness outside. He wondered if it was real or imagined.

"Chilly in here," the usher said, blowing on his knuckles.

"Yeah. Like a tomb," King said with a wry smile.

The usher made no comment and King went to find Gore.

Gore was standing on the stage shouting lighting directions to the booth at the back of the auditorium. He could have used the intercom, but when Gore ran a show he wanted everybody to realize it. Behind him stood a waist-high platform, eight feet long and draped in floor-length black velvet with long candles in ornate candlesticks at each end. It was for Diamond's casket. A freezer encased in dark wood that worked very well.

Gore had experimented by filling it to capacity with bricks of ice cream and, turned up to only half power, it had kept the bricks hard enough to bend spoons. When they emptied the casket to put Diamond in, Gore started giving bricks away but stopped when he realized people would pay for ice cream that had been kept frozen in the same box that held the remains of Johnny Diamond. He stashed the ice cream in another freezer, waiting for the doors to open.

The lighting man was having trouble getting the right combination of spots on the platform. Gore found fault with every possible variation. Green and yellow would make it look like Diamond had a liver infection. Green and red made it look too much like Christmas, and red and blue too much like a brothel. Plain white was too austere. It would make Diamond look dead.

"He is dead, Gore," King said, stepping from the shadows into the light on the stage.

"Damn it, of course he's dead," Gore snapped. "But we don't

want them to know that." He made a great sweeping gesture with his arm, presumably to indicate the mass of humanity.

"I think they already do know," King said, thinking of the thousands of lines of newspaper copy that had been dedicated to the occurrence.

Gore sighed deeply and shook his head. "Of course they know," he said softly. "But when they come in here tonight, all shapes and sizes, all ages, sexes, and colours, with their tear-stained hankies clenched in their trembling hands, I want them to be able to look down at Johnny Diamond, at perhaps the last pure, untarnished idol of this badly tarnished age, and I want them to feel a glimmer of hope, faint as it might be. I want them to feel that maybe, while they watch, he'll just sit right up in that coffin and give them a big wink and leap over the side, taking the microphone and giving them the concert of their lives."

Gore placed a hand on King's shoulder. "You see, King, hope is what we're dealing with here. We're just trying to give these people something to pray for. Some spark of light in the great black firmament of life. Hope that something beautiful hasn't really died after all." King was almost sure he could see tears in Gore's eyes.

Suddenly, Gore pulled back and swung towards the lighting booth, yelling, "Okay, you dumb bastard, let's try and get it right this time. I want something mellow and laid-back, but not catatonic. Jumping Jesus H. Christ, I could do better with a flashlight than you're doing with those spots, you son of a bitch."

King retreated backstage.

Devereaux was lurking there. He nodded at King and came over to him. "Everything's going very well, King," he said.

"Seems to be. Gore's having a field day."

"He's very excited. This is a very exciting project. Nothing like it has ever been attempted before."

"Freezing people? Sure it has."

"Yes, but we are not merely freezing someone. We are preserving for posterity a legitimate and important slice of twentieth-century popular culture."

"Sure. And making a few bucks on the side."

Devereaux smiled. "A mere consequence of our enterprise, King. And don't be so self-righteous. You take just as much as we do. And don't ever forget, Gore and I don't need you. We could drop you in a second and there'd be a hundred other publicists clamouring for your job. Always remember that. You need us."

"Maybe so, but there's something you shouldn't forget either. You both need Diamond. How's it feel to rely totally on a corpse?"

Devereaux smiled his empty smile. "You can count on them," he said. "They never do anything you don't expect."

One cold son of a bitch leading another, King thought, the feeling growing that Diamond, Gore, and Devereaux deserved one another.

To King, it was a difference of degree. He got paid to do a job, but he didn't own a percentage of the body. The thought had crossed his mind that if Gore and Devereaux ever severed their partnership they'd have to divide their assets with a hacksaw. Then, while Diamond's head was playing Poughkeepsie, his genitals would be on display in South Bend, Indiana. "Just make sure he doesn't thaw out, Doc," King said, walking away.

∽

The show went every well. Gore finally decreed the lighting was acceptable, and the doors opened just half an hour late. There was some grumbling from the lineup, which now stretched for blocks, that it was probably all a hoax and Diamond wasn't really dead at all, but nobody left.

Once the doors were open, they streamed in for hours, moving past the blown-up photographs of landmark events in Diamond's career and the collection of memorabilia in glass-covered cases set up in the lobby. Then it was into the auditorium itself, suitably dim as befitted a place of mourning. Filing down the right-hand aisle, they climbed the steps to the stage, where Diamond lay in frozen state.

Each spectator was allowed five seconds' peering down at the star's icy face before being moved along by two burly guards. All through the

49

evening, recordings of Diamond's greatest hits boomed from the speakers, even outside so those still waiting could hear. The music, however, was interrupted frequently by Gore, admonishing the crowd to have patience. After all, Diamond was in no hurry to go anywhere.

By the time the last fan had been ushered out the door, Gore was ecstatic. The evening had gone smoothly. Lighting and sound problems had all been ironed out and crowd control had been the only real concern. Five people, two of them female, had tried to climb into the coffin with Diamond, but the guards restrained them with a minimum of violence. Aside from those few isolated and minor incidents, there had been no trouble.

King found Gore in the lobby rubbing his hands with pleasure.

"Did you see them, King?" Gore asked with a chuckle.

"I saw them."

"We made a killing."

"That's a good thing to call it."

Gore chuckled again. "And it's going to be like this for the whole tour. The extended tour."

It certainly looked, at the outset, like it would be. For the first month the crowds were phenomenal. In every city, they lined up for blocks.

Near catastrophe struck once when a harassed baggage clerk accidentally put Diamond on the wrong flight, and sent Gore and his entourage merrily on their way with the body of a butcher named Stanley Minsky. Fortunately, the error was discovered in time, and a few frantic phone calls averted potential disaster. But the novelty began to wear off after a while. Crowds grew thinner and the media no longer gave Diamond the coverage or hype Gore felt the show deserved. King did the best he could, but found his own enthusiasm waning as quickly as the media's.

Gore grew moody and petulant, snapping at anyone on the slightest provocation. Devereaux remained as outwardly calm as ever. Diamond showed no signs of thawing out or rotting and the doctor was pleased that his job was well taken care of, although some concern had been generated by the appearance of a slight freezer burn on one of

Diamond's cheeks. But a careful application of cosmetics solved that problem.

Gore would pace endlessly backstage as the steadily thinner crowds straggled past his exhibit and mutter to himself as he tried to calculate a new approach. It came to him one night in a dream.

"Diamond will live again," he proclaimed to King with a whimsical smile.

"Huh?" King wondered if the slump in business had finally affected Gore's mind.

"I had a vision last night. The whole show is too static. It needs to be punched up, given a shot of pizzazz. Something to bring the people back and get those media bastards climbing all over one another for stories and pictures."

"What do you have in mind?" King was almost afraid to ask.

Gore just smiled. "You'll see. The new Flawless Johnny Diamond show debuts in a week." He walked away humming to himself. King shuddered with trepidation.

King hadn't slept all night. Watching the chill dawn of the day Gore had promised to rock the entertainment industry a second time, he felt cold. The snow was ankle deep on the sidewalk and continuing to fall. By seven o'clock, the crowd outside the theatre was larger than any King had seen in weeks. Gore's maddening secrecy on television, on radio, and in the press had had the desired effect.

King slipped in the back door and could have sworn he hadn't gone inside. The whole building was like ice. Gore, wrapped in a fur coat and gloves and breathing steam, met King backstage.

"What happened to the furnace?" King asked, hands deep in his overcoat pockets.

"It's been shut off."

"Shut off? What the hell for? It's twenty below out there."

"We had to turn it off. To keep the goods fresh."

"Goods?" King had an image of Gore's new concept being to turn the place into a giant cold cellar full of Diamond's favourite preserves.

"Yes. To keep Diamond solid."

"Diamond? What about the box?"

Gore just smiled and led King to the wing where he could look out over the stage.

Dressed in the sequined silver lamé suit he had made famous, Johnny Diamond stood like a department store mannequin at centre stage. The lights cast alternate ghastly colours on his skin, so obviously pale behind the make-up.

King looked at Gore in horror. "What is this?"

"Quite ingenious, really." Devereaux had crept up behind them on crepe-soled shoes and oiled limbs. He startled King. Walking over to Diamond, he said, "He is held up by a thin but very sturdy wire stand which is hidden inside his suit. Legs, back, chest, and arms." He ran a hand up and down Diamond's leg and caressed his belly like a lover. "Feel it for yourself."

King's stomach turned over. "No."

Devereaux smiled. King could have sworn his teeth all ended in sharp points.

"And this isn't where it ends, King," Gore said, excitement in his voice. "The suit's insulated and lined with tiny refrigeration units to help keep him on ice. But wait till you see the best part."

King wasn't sure he wanted to, but Gore waved both arms to the booth at the back and Diamond suddenly lurched into a grotesque twist while the sound system belted out his cover of an old Chubby Checker hit.

"Good God," King said.

"Isn't it great?" Gore cried, his hands raised before him.

Diamond began a passionate boogaloo as a new song started, strangely out of character with the lifeless aspect of his face.

"The wire does it all electronically," Devereaux explained. "It keeps time, causing Diamond to dance. It's a little jerky, not American Bandstand quality, but certainly more entertaining than having him just lie there and look dead. Care to see him frug?"

"I think I'm going to be sick," King said, turning away.

"Don't go, King." Gore put a hand on King's shoulder. "This is the hope I was talking about. People will once again be able to see their idol dancing and performing before them. He has been raised from the dead for one farewell tour. One last great effort for his devoted fans. What you see before you now is only the beginning. By next week there'll be a backup band."

"That's nuts," King said. "What band in their right mind is going to want to play backup to a rock and roll corpse?"

"The kind of band we have won't mind," Gore said.

"And how the hell much do you have to pay them to play second fiddle to a stiff?"

"Nothing at all," Devereaux said with a smile.

King realized then what they had in mind. A dead band for a dead star. "Oh, no," King said, backing away. "This is where it ends for me." He turned away from Gore and Devereaux, ignoring their protests, and went out the back door, leaving the corpse doing the monkey to an audience of empty seats.

〜

From a coffee shop across the road, King watched the crowds file in. After an hour and no diminishing of number, he left and trudged back to his hotel room, his decision made.

That night, after the show, King returned to the theatre. Gore was saving on hotel bills by storing Diamond in a room backstage, guarded of course, but still cheaper than the two-bedroom suite Diamond always insisted on. King had no trouble getting into the room. The guards were the same two who had been at the door of Diamond's house the night he died the first time, and they knew King.

Inside the room, King worked quickly. He raised the lid of the freezer and caught his breath. Diamond seemed to be watching him suspiciously. Ignoring the glassy stare, his hands turned numb with cold and fear, King maneuvered the rigid corpse free. Opening the single small window, he dumped the body, with much swearing and very little ceremony, into the alley behind the building. Straightening his tie and taking a deep, calming breath, he left the room.

53

Backing his car into the alley, King picked Diamond up and some-how managed to stuff him into a trunk designed to hold little more than a spare tire. At dawn he was four hours from the city and Diamond was in the heated trunk thawing out like one hundred and eighty pounds of hamburger.

At noon, Gore was in the theatre lobby with Devereaux. Both men looked tense and upset. King walked up and they looked daggers at him.

"I want to talk to you, King," Gore said, turning to walk into the auditorium. King followed and Devereaux brought up the rear.

They took seats in the centre of the great empty auditorium, the three of them side by side with King still in the middle.

"Where's Diamond, King?" Gore asked when they were sitting.

King shook his head. "Out of your reach now, Gore."

"I don't think so, King," Devereaux said with the soft, svelte tones he used when he was trying to be convincing. "I don't think you can keep him from us."

"I do. Because I don't have him anymore."

"What the hell does that mean?" Gore demanded.

"Just that. I had him, but I don't any longer."

"Who does?" Devereaux asked with a fatherly smile, although to King he didn't look like he could ever be anyone's father.

"No one."

"How's he staying frozen?"

"He's not. I've buried him."

"Buried him!"

"It wasn't easy with the ground as hard as it is, but I finally got it done."

Devereaux's eyes went wide and Gore slumped back in his seat, shaking the whole row. "You mean he's thawing?"

King nodded. "Slowly, but surely."

"Where is he, King? We have to get him back. He's bread and butter for a hell of a lot of people." Gore turned to Devereaux. "Will he be too far gone?"

Devereaux shook his head. "I don't know. Name your price, King."

"There's no price."

"Where is he, King?" Gore asked, and the way he looked, King knew he would dig Diamond up with his bare hands if he had to. King could see Gore kneeling on the ground in a soiled three-piece suit, face streaked with sweat, scrabbling in the dirt with cracked, blackened nails, fingers, raw and bleeding. Like some crazed, desperate prospector lost in the desert without food or water but still seeking the great, rich vein.

"I'm sorry, Gore," King said, rising, "but Diamond gave you enough while he was alive. He was a bastard, but he's dead now and you've got no right to make him stand up and twitch like a spastic mannequin in front of a bunch of slobbering ghouls just so you can make a buck. I should've done this months ago. This show is over. Find yourselves a live star." He squeezed past Devereaux to the aisle.

"Think it over carefully, King," Devereaux said. "We can make things very uncomfortable for you. And believe me, we will. Unless you tell us where he is. Then we'll pretend this never happened."

"Go to hell."

"Have a heart, King," Gore said, his voice high-pitched in pleading. "What the hell am I going to do with four back-up musicians and nobody to back up?"

King sneered. "Drop dead," he said, and turned away from them.

As he walked towards the back of the auditorium, Gore said to Devereaux, "What do we tell the people?"

"Tell them Diamond's not feeling well and can't go on tonight. We'll think of something."

They did.

The next day, King read in the paper that Bobby "Ace" Freeman had died of an apparent heart attack following a performance the night before. Two weeks later he opened in Vancouver.

Dead Meet

How are we gonna do this?" Thomson asked from the front passenger seat. "Are we gonna fix his brakes so it'll look like an accident?"

"Don't be an idiot," Kelly replied. "We're going to walk up behind him and shoot him in the back of the head."

"That's what we always do," Thomson said with a frown.

Kelly saw a sign for their exit a kilometre ahead and slowed down to the limit, signalling as he eased the car across three lanes of traffic and onto the ramp. "We always do it," he said, "because it always works."

Off the highway, Kelly steered into a wealthy residential district with the houses set well back from the road. Eighty-year-old trees rose up on every front lawn and each private drive boasted two cars, usually European.

"Nice neighbourhood," Thomson said. "They said he's lived around here all his life?"

Kelly nodded.

"I hope he appreciated it," Thomson went on.

Kelly shrugged. "Well, he probably figured on dying here too. So at least we won't be disappointing him."

Kelly drove slowly through the quiet streets, careful to observe all the traffic laws. He came to complete stops, signalled every turn, always stayed at or just below the speed limit. Thomson was amused by how differently Kelly drove when he was on a job than when he wasn't.

"There's his place," Kelly said as they crept past a stone and ivy house which sprawled on a quarter acre of land, half hidden behind pine trees and maples. Kelly checked his watch. "It's nine twenty-three. He should be walking westbound in two minutes. Let's go meet him." Kelly kept driving east and, a couple of hundred yards down the road, they saw a man walking towards them with an athletic bag in his hand.

"It's nice when they co-operate with you like this," Kelly said. "Makes it so much less complicated." Kelly stopped the car and got out. "Excuse me," he said as he crossed the street.

The man stopped and turned to face Kelly, involuntarily swinging the athletic bag in front of him, as if for protection. "Yes?" His voice was strong and confident. Kelly looked at him closely to make sure he was the one. Kelly matched the face against the one he had in his memory: the square chin, the slightly crooked nose, the close-cropped silver hair, the high forehead.

"I seem to be lost," Kelly said. Then he mentioned the address he was looking for. He gave it just enough of that feeling all men have, that having to ask directions is a sign of weakness. "Could you, uh…"

The man smiled and relaxed. "Sure," he said. "Go down here to the second stop sign, turn right, then take the first left."

Kelly smiled too. He couldn't hear it, but he knew that Thomson was out of the car now and had his pistol in his hand. Kelly casually slipped his hand into his overcoat pocket and took hold of his 25 milli-metre Beretta. "Thanks," he said. "And goodbye."

The man nodded and turned away to continue walking home. Thomson was across the street in four quick strides, raising his gun as he moved. Kelly's pistol slipped clear of his pocket and the two of them stepped rapidly up behind the man with the short silver hair. It happened so quickly that by the time he sensed something and started to turn to look the two pistols were resting just inches from his head. They fired almost simultaneously, two soft silenced hacks in the night, and the man pitched onto the lawn of his neighbour's home.

Kelly put his pistol back in his pocket.

"Can I take the gym bag?" Thomson asked.

"Don't be an idiot," Kelly said and walked back to the car.

〜

They were sitting in an English-style pub having a pint of Smithwick's when Thomson asked, "How come we always do it like that?"

Kelly was busy checking out the women in the bar, paying particular attention to a blonde with tight black jeans and high leather boots. "Do what like what?" he asked absently.

"You know," Thomson said. "Do this like this." He made a pistol with his thumb and forefinger, reached up and placed the tip of the extended finger against the back of his head and brought the thumb down while his lips framed a silent gun shot.

Kelly shook his head. "What am I going to do with you? How can anyone so proficient be so stupid? For eighteen months I've been telling you, we do it this way because this is a business. I'm a businessman. And it makes the most business sense. We do it this way because if anything's going wrong we can stop it and try again later. We do it this way because it's simple. There's less for them to trace. We shoot the guy, we dump the guns in the lake where they'll never find 'em. We do it this way because there are no mistakes. You want to put a bomb in somebody's phone, then call up and set it off? You think like a stupid terrorist. I don't know about you, but I don't get paid to blow up somebody's housekeeper, which is just as likely to happen. Me, maybe I'm old fashioned, but when I'm hired to do a job, that's all I want to do. I don't have the stomach for taking out bystanders, unless it's absolutely necessary."

Thomson held up his hand. "I get the point."

"No," Kelly said, shaking his head, "I don't think you do. My point is that the simpler it is the safer it is. We don't have to break in anywhere. We don't have to take the risk of fooling with his car. We don't have to get into messing with explosives or bribing anybody. Plus, they're going to know what happened anyway. The fewer things we touch, the less chance we'll get nailed."

"You don't think it could be made to look like an accident?"

"Never seen it done yet." Kelly turned his attention back to the people at the bar. "Now where the hell did that blonde go?" he muttered.

∽

Kelly sat in his car waiting for Thomson and getting more upset by the minute. Thomson was now eleven minutes late. They had an appointment with a small time building contractor who liked to jog after dark. For some reason that eluded Kelly, the fool took a route through a large park in a ravine that bisected the city. Kelly hoped he enjoyed the first half of the trip tonight, because the last half was going to be murder. Kelly chuckled to himself at the joke, then swore as he looked at his watch again. If Thomson wasn't here within three minutes they'd miss their chance. Kelly knew how long the drive would take, he knew how long they'd have the target in their sights but no one else's. And he knew it was calling for heavy rain later on, which appealed to him. He didn't want to delay. As if to remind him of the time, thunder rumbled in the distance.

Then Thomson was there. He opened the car door and slipped in. "Let's go," he said.

"You're *very* late," Kelly told him as he turned the engine over.

"Sorry," Thomson said without sounding it.

That was it. No apology. No explanation. As he pulled into traffic, Kelly wondered, not for the first time, if it was a mistake to go any further with Thomson. After a year and a half and over thirty business deals, Thomson still had this bizarre notion that you could make a game of it. Kelly had been unable to convince him otherwise. At first, the partnership had seemed like a good idea. Kelly the veteran, the pro, taking a very promising kid and moulding him. Much as he never wanted to work that hard, Kelly envied fathers who could take their sons into the family business. Kelly didn't have a son, no kids at all that he knew of, and admittedly the business was a little bit on the outside, but he'd thought maybe Thomson could fill that surrogate role. He'd never told that to

Thomson, of course. As they drove, he began to feel that maybe it was time for a little infanticide.

"What's on your mind?" Thomson asked after they'd been driving in silence for several minutes.

"Just business," Kelly said. "Like we have a window of opportunity with this guy…"

Thomson laughed. "Window of opportunity? Christ, you gotta stop reading the business section, man."

Kelly ignored him. "We got this time, like eight minutes, when we can be pretty much guaranteed it'll be safe. But because you were so damn late what we don't have is time to be there early, check it out, pick our spot, get ready to do business. Now what we're going to have to do is pull up, get out of the car, get the deal done, and then clear out. I'm telling you if anything smells the tiniest bit off to me, we're giving it a pass tonight. Then it's going to piss down rain a little later and tomorrow there'll be mud everywhere so we won't be doing it tomorrow. And that'll make the other guys we're dealing with a little miffed, which I can't blame them. So that's what I'm thinking about."

"You know, Kelly, you worry too much."

"Do I?"

"Yeah." Then Thomson chuckled. "You think we could make this one look like an accident?"

As it happened, everything went smoothly. They arrived at the place Kelly had chosen in advance. A public parking area where their tire marks and foot prints would be unremarkable. Then they walked along the asphalt path to a point where it bent around a large clump of bushes. They stood there until they could hear the soft pat-pat of jogging feet and louder panting. They both stepped back to the edge of the path, hidden in the bushes' shadow. The jogger came around the bend and was past them before he grew aware of their presence. By then it was too late.

Kelly dropped Thomson off outside his apartment. "I told you, you worry too much," he said.

Kelly just grunted and went home.

The next morning, he had breakfast at a small restaurant he liked run by Greeks. After the residue of the bacon, eggs and toast had been cleared away he sat over coffee thinking at length about what to do. There was another deal coming up out of town, and then one locally, and after that nothing was booked for several weeks. Finally, he drained the last of his coffee, left one of the generous tips which made the Greeks like Kelly's being there as much as he did, and left with the decision made. He would take Thomson out of town with him, then work with him again back home. And then he would dissolve the partnership.

When they were out of town, Thomson suggested trying poison or electrocution. But they used their pistols instead. It was pouring rain and they had to wait for over half an hour for the deal to go down. Kelly was almost ready to call it off, but then their appointment showed up and they left him in an alley with two bullet holes in his head and the rain water filling his open mouth. On the way home, they dropped the pistols in the river.

Three days later it was time to go to work again.

"Be on time," Kelly said. "And don't make any stupid suggestions."

"Don't worry," Thomson said. "I think I'm starting to get the message."

"I'm taking my car in for the 10,000 click service, but it'll be ready by two. I'll pick you up at half past."

Thomson nodded and sneezed.

"Bless you," Kelly said.

Thomson was late the next day. He didn't show and he didn't show and finally Kelly went into a phone booth and called. The voice that answered was hardly recognizable.

"Thomson?" Kelly asked. "Is that you?"

"Yeah," Thomson said, in a thick rasp.

"What's wrong?"

"I'm sick. Standing around in the rain waiting for that son of a bitch. I got a cold like you wouldn't believe."

"Well take something and let's go," Kelly snapped.

"No way, man. I'm not going anywhere except to bed. I'll be useless to you."

"Fine, I'll take care of it myself. I'll call you tomorrow." He hung up the phone. "Idiot," he said to himself as he left the phone booth and got in the car.

He looked at his watch. The meeting was going to take place out in the suburbs. An hour's drive at that time of day. He swore to himself and gunned the engine.

༄

Kelly was in the habit of reading the obituaries every morning, before anything else. He claimed that making a business out of death made him interested in all its forms. It was one of the few of Kelly's habits which Thomson had picked up.

It was two days later that Thomson saw the death notice in the paper. "Died suddenly," it said. "Body to be cremated... donations in lieu of flowers … friends may call..." and gave the address of a prestigious funeral home. Thomson went later that day.

The reception room in the funeral home was deserted except for an attractive redhead about Thomson's age who introduced herself as Kelly's widow. Thomson hadn't even known Kelly was married. He looked her over appraisingly and figured she'd need a lot of consoling.

"I was sorry to hear about your husband," Thomson said.

"Yes," the redhead replied. "It was a terrible shock. He'd just had the car checked and was rushing to a business appointment. No one can understand how the brakes could have failed."

"Accidents happen," Thomson said gently.

She nodded then touched his arm. "Would you like to see him?"

"Pardon?"

"It's an open coffin." She smiled sadly. "That crazy Irishman. It was something he insisted on."

Thomson went up to the far end of the room where the coffin stood. He hesitated, then peered in. Kelly looked up at him and smiled. "Never seen it done yet," he said, raising his pistol and blowing a bullet into one of Thomson's startled eyes. As the body fell, Kelly said, "Idiot," softly, almost to himself.

Advertising Hell

W hat I want," the devil said, "is a damn good ad campaign. You know, something right up there with those TV commercials the Mormons do."

He was sitting on the sofa in Mason's office, his feet up on the coffee table. It was well after six and most everyone had gone home. De Vries had asked Nikki to stay late because they were meeting a potential new client, but he didn't tell her who the client was. The appointment was written in the book as *New Biz Pitch*.

As soon as the devil was seated, Nikki came in and offered something to drink. The devil asked for coffee. Black. No sugar. Nikki brought it to him and he watched her as she walked away. When the door had closed behind her, he turned back to Mason and de Vries. "Real nice butt," he said. "She seeing anybody?"

"Living with someone," Mason said.

The devil sighed. "Ah well. I'm too old for her anyway. Shall we talk business, gentlemen?"

"Before we get into this," de Vries said, "what do we call you? Satan? Lucifer?"

The devil chuckled. "You can call me Lou," he said. "It's more friendly that way."

Since Mason was a child, he'd had an image of what Satan must look like. Like many people, he had envisaged horns and a tail and cloven hooves. But the fellow sitting on his sofa looked more like a stock broker or a brand manager for Procter & Gamble. His hair was moussed and cut short. If he had horns they must have been very small. He had just enough tan to look healthy but not enough to make you start thinking melanoma. He wore a casual cotton suit that did not seem to wrinkle. He did not wear suspenders.

He crossed his legs at the knee and his hands, which were surprisingly delicate, moved expressively as he spoke.

The only pointy things about him were his western boots. But, to Mason, they indicated that the devil had a narrow foot. There was no way a hoof would fit. At least not comfortably. And, lounging on the sofa with his left arm stretched along the top of the back cushions, Lucifer looked nothing if not comfortable.

"I'll be blunt," the devil said. "I need serious marketing help. I'm losing share of mind. It's amazing how many people either don't believe in Hell any more or never heard of us in the first place. Those who do know about us don't see us as a prime destination. We did a study last year and we ranked behind Nigeria and Bosnia and Iraq. So what I have for you is a very big challenge." He smiled again and his tone softened, "Or, as you ad people like to say, a big opportunity."

"I have extensive research here." He pulled a few very thick reports out of his briefcase and dropped them on the coffee table with a whump. "Tracking studies that show our steady decline over the past fifty years. I've even got one study on the public perception of me. Because it's hard to separate me from the brand. It's like that Colonel and the chicken. You know what people think? They still think of me as having horns, hooves and a tail. See what I'm up against?"

Mason shifted in his chair.

"First, let me tell you what I think I need. And then you give me feedback, all right?"

De Vries made his "okay by me" gesture and Mason nodded.

Lucifer counted the items off on his slender fingers. "I need an advocacy campaign. Something to change how people perceive me. Work on the old image. The oil companies do it. The tobacco companies do it. The chemical companies do it. I want to do it. I need a response campaign. Something to get people to take action. To get them to think about coming to Hell before they think about going to Heaven. I need to be top of mind.

"I want to run some promotions. Giveaways. I want to give away free weekend packages. Get people to spend a weekend in Hell. Show 'em what a great place it is. Then they can go home and talk it up. I need that kind of word of mouth working for me."

"Excuse me," de Vries said, "can you do that? Bring people down to Hell for the weekend, and then send them home?"

Lucifer smiled again. His teeth weren't quite perfect. And they were stained slightly yellow. It was another thing that disoriented Mason. It made the devil seem so normal.

"Of course I can do it," he said quietly. "I'm the devil. Now where was I? Oh yeah. I want to get into sponsorship. I want to sponsor public television. I want to sponsor opera. I want to sponsor a whole bunch of things. Car races. I want rink boards in the Stanley Cup playoffs. Right in front of the penalty box.

"And I want people to understand that getting into Hell is a lot like a frequent flyer program. You don't do one thing and it's hey, come on down. It's a process. You build up points and when the time comes you cash 'em in. And it's a whole lot better than return airfare to Hawaii."

"You want to do this just in Canada," de Vries asked, "or...?"

"All over the world," Lou said. "I want a web site on the Internet. I want to be on TV, on radio, in all the big magazines. *Time, Playboy, Newsweek, Ladies Home Journal.* All of 'em. I want an infomercial. Everything that's possible, I want to do."

De Vries drew in his breath. "This will cost you a huge amount of money."

Lou spread his hands wide. "Money," he said, "is no object." And he laughed loudly and for a long time.

∽

The call tipping off Mason and de Vries to the potential new client had come a week before, completely out of the blue. It was from a man named Kevin who'd made his reputation running one of the hottest ad agencies in the country, selling it out to a multinational for big dough. After that he ran a series of smaller, short-lived outfits, each less successful than the one before. Now he made a tidy living helping big clients conduct new agency searches.

"I've got a hot one for you," Kevin said to de Vries the previous Monday morning.

"Who is it, Kevin?"

"Can't tell you. But you want to meet this guy. This could be big."

"How big, Kevin?"

"To paraphrase John Lennon, bigger than God."

Mason and de Vries were intrigued. They'd both been around for years. Building careers at Thompson and Scali and McCann. Then they took up the gauntlet as Co-Creative Directors at Grossman & Roberts, a solid and established firm trying to upgrade its creative reputation. The two owners were legendary for their endless interference and tinkering. Their staff turnover was high. Their advertising came with the slight hint of mothballs, as though it had been stored in a trunk since the fifties. But Mason and de Vries believed change was coming. And that they were the delivery boys.

The two owners, however, proved incapable of backing off. Their stranglehold on the agency persisted. In the end, there were shouting matches that began behind closed doors and soon erupted into the hallways. There were tears from junior art directors. There was heavy drinking among the account people. Once, in expressing his opinion of a television storyboard being presented by an enthusiastic young writer, Grossman took out a lighter and set the piece of paper on fire. He left the writer frantically stomping on the burning commercial, trying to keep the carpet from catching. Two weeks later, someone threw a computer keyboard at Roberts, just missing him and shattering a plate glass window.

Almost exactly a year after they began, Mason and de Vries left Grossman & Roberts and set up their own shop. A month after they'd opened the doors, two of Grossman & Roberts' biggest accounts followed them.

As a result of the defections, there were hirings and parties of celebration and bonuses at Mason & de Vries.

At Grossman & Roberts, however, there were layoffs and wage cuts. Homes were lost. Livers and marriages were damaged past repair. There were lawsuits and counter suits. But ultimately there was nothing the old agency could do. Mason & de Vries was the hottest ad shop in the country. Business came knocking on the door.

And now here was Kevin. Sitting on the sofa with a Scotch in one hand and a cigar in the other, telling the two men that the devil wanted them to pitch his account.

"Come on," Kevin said, when Mason and de Vries expressed hesitation. "You guys love a challenge. What's bigger than this? Compared to doing this job, selling smokes is like selling motherhood."

De Vries shook his head. "This has got to be a joke."

Kevin reached into his briefcase and took out a thick, elegantly bound document. He stood up and walked it across to de Vries' desk. "Here's a Dun & Bradstreet report. Those guys don't joke. Especially about money. Take your time. Check it out. This guy is for real. Just like your mama and Father O'Leary always told you. And he's so damn rich he makes the *Fortune 500* look like pikers. Not just one of them, mind you, but all of them combined. So read up. Think it over. And call me when you decide you're interested. I'll be waiting downstairs in my car."

"Why us?" Mason asked.

Kevin shrugged from the doorway. "Every account in the fucking world is sniffing around you. Why not one from the underworld, too?"

Kevin didn't have to wait in his car for long.

∽

Before meeting with the devil for the first time, they spent three days poring over the D&B reports. The whole time, the question tugged at Mason's mind: "Why us?"

"Because we do great work." De Vries was less concerned about the ramifications of having Satan as a client than Mason was.

69

"Lots of people do great work. He could have anybody. He could take one of the big multinationals and have an agency in fifty countries. We don't even have a PR component. It just doesn't make sense."

"You know what, pal? You think too much. You analyze too much. You want to think about something, think about this. What do they say, there are three reasons to take a piece of business. Money. Fun. Prestige. Pick any two. Well this is one time, pal, when we don't have to settle for two out of three."

"You think this guy's on the level?" Mason asked. "This doesn't feel right. I mean, we've worked for some hellish people in our time, but this guy's in another league."

"Don't worry. We'll do due diligence on him. If he's as rich as Kevin says he is, this is going to be bigger than McDonald's. Bigger than Disney. Imagine fifteen percent of that, my friend. We're going to have to staff up."

So now they were sitting with the devil, talking about making a deal.

"This is going to cost you hundreds of millions of dollars," Mason said.

The devil reached into his inside jacket pocket and took out a cheque. He handed it to de Vries. "I can give you the first six months fees up front as a show of good will."

De Vries showed the cheque to Mason. It was drawn on one of the country's largest chartered banks for a very large amount. "How could you be so sure we'd take your business?" de Vries asked, slipping it into his pocket.

"Let's just say, I have faith in people." He rose smoothly and adjusted his jacket. He continued talking as Mason and de Vries walked him to the elevator. "Study the research. Consider any fee structure you would like. Then get word to me, and we'll begin the strategic process."

"How do we reach you?"

"For now, through Kevin. And I would ask that, for the time being, you keep any mention of this strictly *entre nous*. I've never done this before and you must understand that I'm somewhat cautious."

The elevator door opened and the devil stepped inside. "Thank you for your time, gentlemen. Good night." He reached out and pushed a button. Just before the door closed he looked into Mason's eyes and said, "Going down."

⌒

The devil arrived for their next meeting with a contract.

Mason and de Vries scanned the document in turn. It looked basic and perfectly reasonable. "We'll have to get our lawyer to look at this," Mason said. "It's standard procedure for us."

The devil understood perfectly. "Of course. You can't just go putting your name to anything."

"We don't have to sign it in blood, do we?" de Vries asked.

The devil responded with the polite smile of someone who's heard the same joke once too often. "Ink will be fine," he said.

⌒

"I just got the contract back," the devil said to de Vries, "and I want to tell you how happy I am that we'll be working together. I have absolute faith in your abilities."

"We're really looking forward to it, too. And we'd like to set up a meeting so you can come and meet the folks who'll be working on your business."

The silence on the other end of the phone line went on for so long that de Vries finally said, "Hello? Lou? You still there?"

"Yes, I'm here. But I must admit I'm somewhat shocked. I naturally assumed that you and Mr. Mason would be handling my account personally. Given the revenue I'll be generating for you — I'll be your largest client by far."

It was de Vries' turn for a moment's silence. "Well, of course we'll be involved in your business, but for the day to day —"

The devil cut him off. "Perhaps I've been too hasty. There were other agencies that I had considered talking to. If you would rather not have my account ..." He let the thought trail off but de Vries got the drift.

Shit, de Vries thought. "No," he said, "no. We definitely want your business. Obviously there's just been a little glitch in communication. We're both reasonable people. I'm sure we can work something out."

"I'm sure we can," the devil said.

～

"You agreed to what?" Mason said.

"He woulda walked otherwise. Did you want me to kiss all his money good-bye before we even started?"

"What about our other clients? The people who've been with us since we opened the doors? Do we just call them up and give them, 'Oh, sorry, you don't get our time any more'?"

"It won't come to that. We've balanced what we have so far. All we need to do is juggle him into the mix like we would any other account."

"This isn't just any other account. We're not dealing with some VP of Marketing at a packaged goods company. This guy's the *real* devil. You have no idea how this is going to go."

De Vries got up and went over to Mason, putting an arm around his shoulder. "It'll work out fine," he said. "And beyond the money, think about the awards. We could win some great hardware with this piece of business. We'll be on podiums all over the place. We've got it made."

"God, I hope you're right."

"I'm always right. You know that." Then he picked up the devil's file. "Grab those research reports, will you? I have the boardroom booked for the afternoon. He wants a strategy in a couple of weeks."

～

For the next two weeks, Mason and de Vries huddled in the boardroom. Their days started early and ran late. De Vries told Nikki to take messages for them - they were not available to anyone. Not to staff, not to clients. She fabricated excuses and cancelled meetings. Meanwhile, staff members were given Mason and de Vries' responsibilities for managing accounts and approving new ads.

The problem the devil faced was more complex than they had imagined. They had to come up with a way of positioning Hell that made it seem like an alternative Disneyland. They had to position the place to appeal to the entire spectrum of the population. But they couldn't make it seem anti-Christian or anti-God. They had to make Hell seem like the place for everyone. They had, they finally decided, to find a way to make Hell seem almost wholesome. But with a bit of an edge.

After the first week, they felt good about the strategy. It was starting to take shape nicely. Outside the boardroom, life wasn't so smooth. By now there was rumbling and rumour in the agency. What are they doing in there? How come we're being kept in the dark? They're going to sell the place. There's going to be a merger. There are going to be layoffs. They've both gone nuts. Nikki was pestered with questions. But all she could do was shrug.

"Mr. de Vries?"

"God damn it, Nikki, I said we weren't to be disturbed."

"But it's really important," Nikki said. "It's Mr. Hightower and he's really pissed off."

Hightower was the Director of Marketing for Cap'n Nemo Seafood, a nation-wide chain of restaurants and a Mason and de Vries client from the beginning. "Tell him I'm tied up and I'll call him back," de Vries said.

"That's what I told him yesterday, and you forgot to call him."

"Damn," de Vries said.

Hightower wasn't the only client who'd called. There were angry messages from Dean McClimond at Dadashi Electronics, Frank Ponsonby at Book Ends and Susan Poad at The Curling Network.

"Call back and tell them I have a big pitch tomorrow. I'll call them after that."

Nikki looked at him doubtfully. "They're not going to be happy."

"Yeah, well, if this pitch doesn't go well, I'm not going to be happy. And if I'm not happy, nobody's happy."

꿍

The pitch didn't seem to go well. It was the first time they had ever been to the devil's office. He had an impressive suite high up in a new tower near the lake. He had told Mason and de Vries that he paid a very favourable rent considering the location. And he had a long term lease.

Mason and de Vries got there half an hour early to set up and work out how best to present in the unfamiliar boardroom. The receptionist showed them in. The room was long and dark with no windows, despite the fact that the view would have been spectacular.

They had pulled together a video showing their best commercials and another one that outlined the capabilities of the agency. The electronics equipment was set up on a stand at the head of the room, but they couldn't get the VCR to work. All that came up on the big TV was static.

They weren't offered coffee. And when the devil finally came in, several minutes late, he was followed by half a dozen associates. Fortunately, Mason had brought extra documents to hand out, so there was one for each of them. But Lou never introduced anyone. He simply sat down at the head of the boardroom table. The associates clustered around him. Three on his left and three on his right. "Begin, gentlemen," he said.

"We have a couple of videos," de Vries said. "But we can't seem to make your equipment work."

The devil shrugged. "Lots of people have that difficulty," he said. "Begin."

Mason and de Vries exchanged looks and went ahead. They were as prepared as they'd ever been in their careers. Every statement they made was supported by facts culled from the supplied research or from additional data that they had dug up on their own. The strategic document had a logical flow that would have made any marketing person nod away like a bobble-headed dog in the back window of a suburban sedan.

The reactions they got from the seven people at the other end of the table were not what Mason and de Vries were used to, however. The audience barely seemed to be paying attention. Only Lou remained focused. The rest of them whispered among themselves, every so often making jokes because peals of laughter blurted out at times when neither Mason nor de Vries had said anything amusing. At significant points in the presentation, one or another of them got up and simply walked out of the room, came back in with coffee - still not offering any to Mason or de Vries - and two or three times took out cell phones and made calls.

Mason and de Vries danced and waved their arms and sold as hard as they could. When they were done, after slightly more than an hour, de Vries asked, "Are there any questions?"

Instead of answering, the seven all stood up at once. "Thank you for your efforts," Lou said. "You have clearly put a lot of thought into it, and it is not all without merit. I'll be back to you later today with some suggestions. I'm sure you can find your way out." Then they all turned and went. Mason wondered if the fact that they all left their handouts lying on the table had any significance.

᭕

"What a bunch of assholes," de Vries said in the cab on the way back.

"It was something to behold," Mason said.

"But we were great, eh?"

"Buddy, we were amazing."

᭕

There was a stack of messages waiting for them when they got back. The production manager wanted to see them. The head of the media buying house they used wanted to see them. Barry, the Director of Client Services, wanted to see them. Two of their biggest clients had called with urgent messages. And the devil had called.

"That was quick," de Vries said. "Do you want to call him, or do you want me to?"

"How did he sound, Nikki?" Mason asked.

"He sounded fine. He asked me out."

"Oh, yeah? You might have to do it to help us get the account."

"I might do it anyway. He looks kinda like Ralph Fiennes."

"He loved it," de Vries said when he put down the phone. "They all loved it."

All the devil had asked for was a little fine tuning - a tweak here or there. He'd get back to them in a few days. Perfect. That gave Mason and de Vries time to do what they knew had to be done. Call the neglected clients. Set up meetings. Go over how business was doing. Start looking at plans for next year.

ꜱ

Mason had just slipped one last file into his briefcase and was putting on his jacket when Nikki buzzed him. "There's a client here to see you."

Mason didn't have anything scheduled. "Who is it?"

"It's Lou. For you and Mr. de Vries. He says it's urgent."

Mason went cold. "Ask him to hang on for a minute. Get him a coffee."

He put the phone down and opened his daytimer. He was sure there was no meeting scheduled. If there was, he knew he'd never let it slip his mind. He flipped to that day. Nothing. They had a meeting set up for the following Tuesday. Go to the devil's office. Get his input. Go away and refine the strategy. But there was nothing before then. The devil was happy with the progress. So he said. He was fine with the schedule. What the hell was he doing in reception? Mason called de Vries. "We've got a problem."

ꜱ

"Of course, I understand," the devil said.

Mason and de Vries both smiled with relief.

"I understand that you don't have time for me." His voice was soft and quiet. "I understand that I am the biggest client you two gentlemen are ever likely to have and yet you place me behind your other clients - a cable television network that takes at least 120 days to pay an invoice; a maker of second rank computer hardware and a chain of remainder bookstores, a perfect growth client for the post-literate age."

Mason started to wonder how the devil knew who they were meeting that day. Then he thought, oh yeah.

"That's not entirely true —" de Vries began.

"Isn't it? I show up here with an emergency - at a time in our relationship when you should be doing everything possible to inspire it to flourish - and you cast me aside."

Jesus, Mason thought. Jesus, Jesus, Jesus. He was getting a headache.

"We have responsibilities to all our clients. We've done nothing but work on your business since we signed the agreement. All that time we were getting ready for the presentation, we did nothing for anyone else. We have to spend some small amount of time with them. Then, once you give us input, we'll get back to work on your account. Now, if we could assign some other people to your —"

The devil held up a hand. "No. Not yet. Only the two of you. Until we get everything up and running, of course. Then we can talk about other people. But for now I insist on absolute secrecy and your total commitment."

Mason's headache was getting worse. "You said something was urgent."

"Yes. A promotional opportunity has just come up and I thought it would be a perfect way to get our relationship off to a flying start."

De Vries tried one last time. "Look, why don't I stay and take the briefing and Mason can go meet with our other clients -"

The devil shook his head. "That won't work. It would be much better to brief both of you together. There's no time to lose. Perhaps your Director of Client Services - that's Barry McIntyre, isn't it? - could fill in for you."

Mason was going to argue more, but de Vries picked up the phone.

The devil smiled. "I'll wait in the boardroom."

~

Two o'clock in the morning. The devil was right. The briefing had been complicated. But the project was different and exciting. Once Mason and de Vries got into it, grappling for a solution that would work, they forgot about the other meetings. Time evaporated.

Late in the afternoon, Barry came back. He stuck his head into the boardroom with his report. All the clients were unhappy to see him instead of the two partners. They all wanted to be called first thing in the morning. There were really bad vibes all over the place. "And I don't suppose you're even going to tell me what the hell you're working on," he said.

"Good night, Barry," de Vries said.

By two thirty they were done. The solution was simple and brilliant and they were both wired. Then the phone rang. "I'm glad I caught you," the devil said.

"We just finished. You're going to love this."

"I'm sure it's very good. Unfortunately, the whole project has been cancelled."

"What?"

"I appreciate all your efforts on my behalf. I wanted to tell you before it got any later. I'll call tomorrow to discuss next steps on the larger strategy." The line went dead.

"Christ," Mason said. "What the hell just happened? There's something wrong here. I'm starting to get a bad feeling. I say we walk away from this."

"We'll talk about it tomorrow," de Vries said.

Heading down to his car, Mason couldn't stop wondering what kind of client kills projects at two thirty in the morning.

~

They lost their first account the following week. Mason had just walked into his office when the phone rang. It was Susan Poad from The Curling Network.

"I called yesterday and left messages for you and de Vries but no one got back to me. Again."

"Didn't Barry call you?"

"Yes, Barry called me. But I didn't want to talk to Barry. I didn't phone and leave a message for Barry. I'm getting sick and tired of talking to Barry. I'm tired of seeing Barry. Barry isn't the one who's been avoiding me."

"No one's been avoiding you, Susan."

"No? Well, I'm just calling to tell you that you don't have to hide from me anymore because I'm putting the account under review."

Mason had not expected this. "Why don't we get together later this morning and talk about this?"

"Too late. Besides, you'd probably just end up sending Barry."

∽

There was nothing Mason loved more than a challenge. The feeling of wrestling with a problem. Turning it around in your brain and looking at it from all sides. Holding it up to the light. Then finally seeing it from an off-kilter angle that still made strategic sense. He loved that more than anything. And he thought he'd solved just about every kind of problem that could be thrown his way. De Vries was the same. So why couldn't they crack this one? He'd had tough clients before. He just needed to find a way to unhinge his mind a little further. There was something there that they just weren't seeing. But they were close. He could feel it. The answer would come soon. It had to. They couldn't afford to ignore their other clients much longer.

∽

"Forget the Bahamas," the devil read aloud. *"Forget Mexico. There's nowhere on*

79

earth as hot as Hell." The devil paused and rubbed his chin. Then he read it again. *"Forget the Bahamas. Forget Mexico. There's nowhere on earth as hot as Hell."*

He was standing in the boardroom looking at a mock-up of a poster mounted on an easel. De Vries stood beside the easel and Mason was sitting at the cherrywood table.

It was two days after the loss of The Curling Network and they were presenting the big campaign. This was the last item on the day's agenda. They'd already gone over changes to the strategy, which the devil seemed to like. Now they were showing the prototype for a series of full-page, four-colour print ads and posters. The images were taken from still photographs the devil had supplied. It was too early in the proceedings to send a photographer down to Hell for a photo shoot.

"I don't know," the devil said, reading the line a third time.

"We did some research," de Vries jumped in. "We picked out the top two places most people think of when they think of hot destinations. Top three really, but we left Florida out. Those people, most of them, aren't in the group we want to target. They probably aren't ready for something as exotic as a week in Hell." Then he laughed, "Actually, Florida's kinda like Hell anyway."

"Not even close," the devil said in a way that made de Vries stop laughing. Then the devil thought about it for a second, and added, "Well, maybe Orlando."

De Vries forged ahead. "See, the line gets a nice double entendre on the word hot. We're saying, 'it's hot,' like warm, hot, sunny. Well, I guess not sunny, but, hey, that could be a good thing. We should do some ads that talk about how it's hot but you don't have to worry about skin cancer. Actually, that could be a big USP. Anyway, so there's that one meaning of 'hot' and then there's 'it's hot.' Like it's the happening place to go. It's where you want to be. It's cool so therefore it's hot. You know? Cool is hot. It's hip."

Lou continued to stare at the poster. "Sorry, guys," he said at last. "It just isn't doing it for me. Now I'm not saying it's bad. Don't get me wrong. There's stuff about it that I like. You're just not quite there yet. I think, too, that

I want to steer clear of that 'high temperatures and open flames' cliche. But hey." He smiled, "You're getting warm."

This was not the news that Mason and de Vries wanted to hear. They had high hopes for this approach. But Lou wasn't about to change his mind.

Six weeks later, his rejections of their work had grown less gentle. By then, Mason and de Vries were in with something even they didn't feel good about. A typical commercial opened with two men stuck in traffic. Tempers are running high and cars are overheating. Then the driver in a 4 by 4 cuts off a sports car driver. The second man yells, "Go to Hell" but the first driver does not respond with the expected angry retort or threatening gesture. Instead, he smiles broadly and says, "Now that's a heck of an idea." The commercial then cuts to many happy scenes of folks frolicking in Hell. Lounging by the sulphur baths. Barbecuing over live coals. Being served drinks by fetching waitresses in red devil costumes.

At the end of the commercial, the offending driver is back at his office where a harried secretary bumps into him. "Go to Hell," he says. She gives him an enveloping smile and replies, "Thanks. That's a heck of an idea."

The music, a new recording of Liszt's *Mephisto Waltz*, swells to a crescendo and the announcer, with a suitably satanic basso-profundo, says, "Go to Hell. You'll have a heck of a time."

The commercials followed one upon the other in predictable fashion. Showing all the age groups and hellish activities. The devil didn't like it. He had trouble with the word heck.

"What is that, heck? What is that?"

"Well, we can't use the word 'hell' again. We can't say, 'Go to Hell. You'll have a hell of a time'. It doesn't sound good. It doesn't work."

"As far as I can see, it doesn't work whether you use the word hell twice or not. I can't understand this. I can't understand why you guys are having so much trouble with this job. But you just don't seem to get it. You remember that testimonial campaign you proposed a month ago? The one that talked about come to Hell and find out who Jack the Ripper really was or have dinner with Vlad the

Impaler or party with Caligula? What was the line that went with that?"

"You never know who in Hell you'll meet," Mason said with none of the heart he'd felt when he first wrote the line.

"Yeah, that was it. Man, I hated that." The devil proceeded to list all Mason and de Vries' failures. The one with John Wilkes Booth and other famous actors reading excerpts from Dante. The humorous approach with Charon sharing amusing anecdotes about some of his more famous passengers. "And that Hellzapoppin' thing with the Busby Berkeley dance routine? Feh." The devil made a disgusted face.

"It's all consistent with the approved strategy," de Vries said, but it wasn't much use.

"Yeah? Well it's consistent all right. Consistently lousy. As far as I'm concerned none of this shit works. I'm damned if I'm going to run some campaign that looks like a string of second rate beer commercials. Get the heck out of here. And come back soon with something I can buy."

～

"That's it," Mason said in the cab. "We resign. Now. Today." He took out his cell phone and held it towards de Vries. "Do you make the call or do I?"

De Vries shook his head. "No."

"You don't want to? I will then."

"Nobody's going to. We're going to redo the work and re-present."

"What? Are you nuts? We're going to cut our losses and dump the account."

"I don't think we can do that."

"Why the hell not?"

"Because we need it. He's paying all his bills. He's firing us a fat monthly retainer, bigger than anything we ever imagined. He's paying hourly for creative development. He's paying mark-ups on all the out of pockets and production. And that's what we need right now. TCN is gone. Cap'n Nemo is gone — "

"What?"

De Vries pulled an envelope from his jacket pocket. "This came in first thing this morning. I didn't figure there was any percentage in telling you before the presentation. One of us knowing was enough."

Mason read the letter twice. It was from Hightower informing them, in his usual terse manner, that they were fired. He was beginning a search for a new agency. He had no intention of considering the incumbent. He was extremely unhappy with the way in which his business, a cornerstone of Mason & de Vries since Day One, had come to be treated. Mason's hand was shaking as he handed the letter back.

"And I got a phone call from McClimond. They're meeting internally at Dadashi tomorrow to discuss replacing us as well."

Next to Hell, Dadashi was their biggest piece of business. Mason leaned his head back on the cab seat. "Jesus Christ," he said.

De Vries put the letter back into his pocket. "So I think we better do whatever the hell Lou wants, don't you?"

ᔕ

Mason tossed that week's issue of *Strategy* on de Vries' desk. "Well, we made the front page again, above the fucking fold." The headline was bold and glaring "What's going on at Mason & de Vries?" That week's issue of *Marketing* was not much different. Speculation was rife. The vibe in the shop was ugly. Mason figured everybody on staff must have their resume out on the street. Other agencies were stalking the accounts that were left like hyenas around a gazelle carcass.

"What did you say to me about fun, money and prestige? Well, this isn't fun anymore. It's painful. And we can't even tell people what we're doing. We're losing business hand over fist. We look like idiots. Where's the prestige in that?"

"So what do you propose?"

"We resign the account. It's not too late to keep Dadashi. I've always had a good relationship with Susan Poad so I'll work on getting The Curling Network back. And you know Hightower. But if we keep going like this, we're going to lose the agency. I know it."

De Vries thought about the invoices, issued like clock work every month and paid with the same monotonous regularity. Then he thought about what would happen if Hell was the only account and Lou decided to change agencies. "All right," he said. "We go tomorrow and tell him to find another shop. I'll get Nikki to call and set up the appointment."

∽

"You don't understand," Lou said the next day. He had kept Mason and de Vries waiting for over two hours in reception. It had been slightly redesigned since their last visit. It was refurnished. The soft leather sofas had been replaced with the folding chairs they both remembered from school assemblies in the gym when they were children. The handle on the inside of the door was gone too. They hadn't realized that, of course, when they went in. The door shut behind them as softly as ever. But when they tried to leave after sitting for thirty minutes, they found that they could not open the door. There was nothing to hold on to. It was like being in the back of a very corrupt police officer's cruiser.

"What is this?" de Vries snapped. "What the hell's going on here?"

"I'm sorry," the receptionist said. "You'll just have to wait."

"We have another meeting."

"I'm sorry," she said and went back to typing, whiting out and retyping.

De Vries looked around for the phone. "Where'd the phone go?" he asked, but she appeared not to hear him.

"Use your cell," Mason said. But, while it had performed perfectly well in the past, all de Vries was able to get on the phone now was a noise that Mason recognized as Lou Reed's *Metal Machine Music*.

"Would you like a coffee while you're waiting?" the receptionist asked politely.

They both nodded but she didn't move. No coffee ever came.

And the clacking of her ancient Underwood upright went on and on and on.

After two hours, they were taken to see Lou. "Obviously," he said the moment they were in his office, "you don't understand."

They weren't asked to sit down. "You can't resign this account." Mason and de Vries looked at one another. Both thought the same thing. I didn't tell a soul what we had planned. My bastard partner must've leaked this. "What are you going to do without it?"

⌇

The elevator door opened and Mason stepped towards it. He hadn't slept much the night before and he wasn't paying attention. Barry came out of the elevator and Mason nearly bumped into him.

Barry was holding an open cardboard box. Mason looked down into it and saw Barry's pencil holder and his wind up toys and the Japanese flag he kept for no reason anyone could figure out.

"Barry, what's this? Where you going?"

"Home, I guess."

Mason looked at his watch. Ten past nine. "Are you sick?"

Barry looked at him angrily. "What the hell kind of a question is that? Am I sick? Yeah I'm sick. I'm heartsick. I left Ogilvy to join you two bastards. 'Oh come on Barry, we need you, Barry.' Big talk. Big promises. So I left and joined you and now look at me. Out on my ass. No notice. I'm the best God damned suit you ever worked with and I get canned like some lousy co-ordinator. Who do you think is going to help you build the agency up again? Nobody in this city's going to want to go near you. My lawyer will have a field day."

Mason was stunned. "What are you talking about? Canned?"

"Yeah, everybody. As soon as he got word about Dadashi. Account's gone. Now the people are gone."

Gone? They'd left it too late. Dadashi spent more than $15 million a year through the agency. Now, because they'd lost focus, been too caught up in Hell, been ignoring every other piece of business, McClimond had pulled the plug. "Who fired you?" he asked, poking the UP button so hard his finger hurt.

"Your pal. De Vries. Tucked away for weeks working on some secret project he won't share with anybody else except you. He doesn't come out of his precious war room from one day to the next and then all of a sudden he's walking around jabbing his finger and it's, 'You and you and you. Don't let the door hit you on the way out.' Well you know what, you guys had a mutiny brewing anyway. Everybody was ready to leave. It was too damn weird what was going on, whatever it was. And you bozos didn't even notice."

Jesus, Mason thought. Jesus Christ. He pounded the elevator button again. "I'm sorry, Barry. I had no idea. I'll see what I can do."

He pushed the button once more, but the elevator refused to come any faster. He ran for the stairs. As the fire door closed behind him he heard Barry's voice call out, "You better hurry. All hell's broken loose up there."

い

The office was a nightmare. People crying. People sitting in stunned silence. People filling boxes and making phone calls. To headhunters, other agencies, lawyers.

Mason found de Vries behind his closed office door. "You fired everybody?"

"Not everybody. I'm keeping Nikki and Phyllis in accounting."

"You didn't talk to me."

"There was no other choice. McClimond fired us."

Mason went and opened de Vries' office door and looked out at the people. "Where is the fun in this?" he asked. "Where is the prestige?"

"The prestige?" Mason had once looked into the eyes of a fundamentalist Christian preacher and when he turned and looked at de Vries he saw the same kind of irrational certainty. "The prestige comes when we announce that we've landed the biggest account the ad world has ever seen. The prestige of having the one piece of business that everybody else on the planet wants. We walk into every ad hangout in town from Betty's to Rodney's to the Courthouse and heads'll be turning to look at us. They'll be asking themselves what we have that got us the hottest piece of business ever. That's prestige. And the money? That's why we started our own shop. But we never dreamed of this much."

"There is no shop anymore. There's just you."

"You and me."

"No. Just you. I've had enough and I'm going home."

~

Mason was very tired. He realized it as he climbed behind the wheel. The stress. Weeks of not sleeping. Late nights. Endless meetings and disappointments. Now the agency gone. He felt empty.

He was almost home, accelerating smoothly around the bend that curved into the last mile of his drive. This was his favourite part of the trip. On his left the ground fell away into a deep ravine. Mason loved to watch the way the trees in the ravine changed almost every day. He was distracted by them now, coated in snow, when his car hit the black ice. He fought for control but it was no use.

The car was a twenty-year-old Mercedes, powerful and strong as a panzer. It smashed past the guardrail and hurtled down the ravine. Inside, Mason was bounced and slammed against the door and the steering wheel. Then a huge tree loomed in front of him and, as it filled the windshield, he shut his eyes and all he could think was, "Thank God I'm off that damned account."

~

Mason opened his eyes and saw the devil staring down at him. Face quite close and smiling. Mason shut his eyes but could still feel the warmth of that smile. Then he opened his eyes again, couldn't see anyone and for a second thought the devil was gone. Then he turned his head and saw Lou on the other side of the room.

"Is this Hell?" Mason asked.

"Only if you eat the food," the devil said. "It's St. Michael's Hospital." The devil was pacing and Mason had trouble following him. His brain felt sluggish and awkward and his eyes kept slipping out of focus.

"So I'm not dead?" There was an IV tube in his arm, a cast on one leg and lots of bandages.

"Oh my, no. Not for some time yet, I'm afraid." The devil moved again.

Trying to follow him, Mason started to get dizzy. "Stand still," he said.

"I can't," the devil said. "If I stand in one place too long the sprinkler system goes off. And this is a new suit. Besides, I don't feel comfortable in here." He pointed to the picture of Jesus on the wall.

"What are you doing here anyway?" Mason asked.

"I came to check on my creative guru."

Mason shook his head, setting it pounding. "You mean former creative guru."

The devil chuckled. "I told you you're not dead yet."

"That's not what I meant and you know it."

Lou reached into his jacket and pulled out a folded sheet of paper. He flicked the paper open with the sound of a cracking whip and held it in front of Mason's wavering eyes. It was the contract, so recently signed. "We have a deal," the devil said.

Mason shook his head. "We went over every inch of that agreement. There's nothing in it about souls. Mine or de Vries'."

"Who's talking about your soul? I'm talking about ads. This piece of paper guarantees that you'll make ads for me in exchange for money. And I've more than kept my part of the bargain." The devil moved close to the bed while he was talking and then walked around it and over to the window and then across to the door and then back to Mason's bedside. Mason's head was swimming.

"I quit. I told de Vries I was through."

The devil smiled. "He'll take you back. Then you two gentlemen are going to work on this until you solve it. And you will. And it will be great. That's why I'm pushing you so hard. That's why I haven't accepted anything you've shown me up till now. But it will happen. Hell's awareness levels will climb right up there with Coke and McDonald's. Market share will soar."

"The only way you could get me to work for you anymore is if we'd done a Faust and signed something in blood."

"Unfortunately, contracts like that don't stand up too well in court. But this one's iron clad." He shook the paper at Mason. "Besides, I don't need that kind of contract to get you."

"What the hell does that mean?"

"You know the kind of results the right ad campaign can achieve. Once you succeed, I'll have almost more souls than I'll know what to do with. I'll be rolling in them. And," he pointed his finger square at Mason's face, "it'll be because of you. How do you think my competition is going to feel about that? Do you think the man upstairs is going to be thrilled with you for making it happen? He's not quite as forgiving as they'd have you believe." The devil moved again. "I don't need your signature to get your soul. You're going to advertise your way to Hell."

Mason met the devil's gaze and knew that it was so. Not damned if you do, but damned when. "Damn," he said.

"Down at the nursing station they told me you'll be here for another few days. That'll give you lots of time to come up with something new." The devil walked to the door. "I've got to go," he said. "The head nurse gets off in fifteen minutes and I'm taking her to dinner. You know what they say about nurses." He left.

For a few brief seconds, Mason swore to himself that he wouldn't do it. Contract or no contract. But before the devil's footsteps had faded away down the hall, the ideas were already boiling up in his head.

This One's Trouble

I know what your trouble is," the short man said.

At first, Bayly wasn't sure if the guy was talking to him or not so he just sat hunched over his beer staring at the rows of bottles behind the bar.

The short man didn't move. "I know what your trouble is," he said again.

This time, Bayly half turned his head, twisting it a fraction on his cartoon character neck. The short man stood maybe ten feet away. He was thin and droop shouldered but his suit looked very expensive and his hair had that fake curled perm look that Bayly found so particularly stupid on men. Bayly looked him up and down, then turned back to the bottles behind the bar and continued trying to determine whether gin was more popular than vodka.

The short man changed tactics. "Do you know what your trouble is?" he asked, using some kind of quasi-psychological approach.

Bayly snorted. Sure, he knew what his trouble was. His trouble was that it was the All-Star Break and he was sitting in a bar in Toronto instead of being at the stadium with the American League team, taking batting practice and gearing up for the game. It was due to start very soon and Bayly wanted to be good and liquored up before the big TV set behind the bar was switched on.

His batting average was hovering dangerously close to the Mendoza Line. He was being platooned for the first time in his career. The

91

hometown fans booed when he came to the plate. And his wife had left him two weeks before, on account of she found out about Janine, and she was after him for a huge settlement. Yeah, Jack Bayly knew exactly what his trouble was.

"Do you mind if I sit down?" the short man asked.

Bayly hesitated, unsure whether he should just pound the guy and get it over with, but then he figured that would just compound his problems so he shrugged instead. The short man sat.

"My name is Henderson," the short man said, holding out a narrow hand which Bayly ignored. "Michael Henderson."

Bayly cast another sideways glance at the short man who returned it with intensity. "I notice that your beer is almost finished. May I buy you another?"

Bayly nodded once.

The short man signaled the bartender. "Another draft beer for Mr. Bayly," he said, "and a Campari and soda for me, please, barman." The bartender set the drinks in front of them as Henderson perched on a barstool one away from Bayly. He raised his glass and smiled. The red liquid looked like soda pop to Bayly and he felt a mixture of contempt and disgust for any man who would drink it. "Cheers, Mr. Bayly. Here's to your good health and continued success."

Bayly snorted. "Don't make jokes where the punchline could get you a shot in the head," he said.

Henderson shook his head vigorously. "I'd be the last one to make jokes at your expense, Mr. Bayly. I'm absolutely sincere. I want to drink to your guaranteed success."

"I've hit three dingers since May and right now I probably couldn't hit a beach ball with a tennis racquet. That ain't my idea of success."

"In baseball terms, no, I'd have to agree with you. But, Mr. Bayly, the tide is about to turn."

Something in the way he said it made Bayly turn his head. Henderson was sitting with a serious, studious expression, his bright eyes blinking behind his glasses. "What the hell do you mean?"

Henderson reached down and lifted a thick black briefcase from the floor at the foot of his barstool. He laid it on top of the bar and rested his hand on it. "In here," he said in a conspiratorial whisper, "I have the root of your trouble. And in here," he tapped his forehead with a thin finger, "I have the solution." He unsnapped the briefcase and opened it to reveal a number of unmarked videotapes. "It's all on these tapes," he said.

Bayly felt momentary panic as he thought about numerous indiscretions with adoring female fans, but then he remembered that his wife was divorcing him anyway. "What you got?" he asked cautiously.

"I have most of your season here, and some of last year's. In all, over three hundred twenty At Bats. I've studied it for hundreds, if not thousands of hours, and I think I know how we can fix things."

Bayly had heard that before. From the manager, the batting coach, his teammates, from a few hundred fans who'd written in suggesting he do everything from use a lighter bat to jump off the CN Tower. And he'd tried a lot of things too. He'd opened his stance and choked up on the bat. He'd taken a shorter stride for a while and then he'd taken a longer one. He'd switched from one batting glove to two then tried it barehanded. Nothing worked. If anything, the situation just got worse.

"What do you think it is?" Bayly asked, taking another sip of beer.

"It's your left wrist," Henderson said with satisfaction.

"Huh? You mean I'm cocking it too much? Johnny Venuti already told me that one."

"It's not what you're doing with the wrist at the plate. It's what you're not doing in general."

Bayly looked at the little man skeptically. "What the hell does that mean?"

"The bracelet."

At first, Bayly didn't get it. Then it slowly dawned. The bracelet was a huge gold chain he'd worn on his left wrist the first five and a half years of his marriage. His wife had given it to him on their wedding day and he hadn't taken it off, except when he was in bed with other women during road trips, until he met Janine toward the end of the previous season and she told him what she thought of jewelry on men.

"I don't know whether it was the weight of that bracelet, the tiny difference it must have made to the timing of your swing, or whether it's just the psychological factor, the way you used to shake it up your wrist before every pitch, but the day you took that bracelet off the wheels came off the wagon, so to speak." Henderson said it as if postulating a scientific theory.

Bayly wasn't much for physics, and he didn't believe that the weight of a hunk of gold jewelry could make that much difference. But he was superstitious. He never stepped on the foul line going on or off the field. He took everything out of the on-deck circle before stepping into it. And he always went on to the field before the second baseman and after the right fielder. He believed in what Henderson was saying, but he wasn't about to admit it.

"Where'd you get those tapes?" he asked.

"From the television," Henderson said.

"That's illegal, ain't it?"

"I won't tell if you won't."

They smiled at one another and then the bartender switched on the game. Bayly wasn't half as drunk as he'd hoped to be but as he watched them introduce the starting line-ups, he found he didn't care as much as he had a while earlier. He and Henderson sat there watching the game together, not speaking. The bar began to fill up and it was the bottom of the third before Bayly turned to comment on a particularly adept play by the shortstop and realized that Henderson was gone.

⌇

A month later, Bayly was on a tear. His average was up sixty points and every time he stood at the plate it looked like the left field fence was only about ten feet away. Pitchers all seemed to be grooving batting practice fastballs right in his wheelhouse. And the team was thriving on it, having soared up the standings so now they were just two games back. But sitting in a bar with four other team-mates, sucking the foam off an imported draft, Bayly was not a happy man.

He was worried about the next series. Four games at home against the division leaders. Four games that could decide the outcome of the season. Bayly was thinking about those four games, paying little attention to his companions, grunting the occasional disinterested response, when he sensed someone standing next to him.

"I know what your trouble is," a voice said.

"Henderson," Bayly said, spinning in his chair and grinning ear to ear. He held up his left hand and shook it, setting the heavy gold bracelet flapping. "I took your advice."

"So I noticed," Henderson smiled. "But there's something else now, isn't there?"

The other players at the table had fallen silent and were looking at Henderson with the suspicion athletes usually reserve for outsiders.

"Let's sit over here," Bayly said, standing up and picking up his beer. They moved to a booth across the bar and as soon as they were a few steps away the other players became as animated as before, Henderson out of their sphere and forgotten.

"Get you a drink?" Bayly asked. "Campari and soda, right?"

Henderson nodded and Bayly signaled the waiter. When the drink arrived, Henderson said again, "There's something else troubling you now, isn't there?" When Bayly nodded, Henderson went on, "And I know what it is." He tapped the big, fat briefcase he again had with him. "In here, I have the root of your problem." He tapped his forehead. "And in here, I have the solution."

"More tapes?"

Henderson nodded. "Of every game you've played in the last two years where Buck Snelgrove was an umpire. He really doesn't seem to get along with you very well, does he, Mr. Bayly?"

Bayly snorted a laugh. "If that ain't the understatement of the year. That son of a bitch hates my guts. He's thrown me out of three games last year. Two already this year. And at the plate..." Bayly just shook his head.

Henderson picked up the story. "His strike zone when you come to the plate is so big you could drive a truck through it and even the wheels wouldn't be called low."

"Damn right. So I go up there, I gotta swing at everything. I struck

95

out three times the last time this guy called a game. And even if he's on the bases I'm not safe. He'll find a way to get me. Had me picked off first last time when my hand was in under the tag. Every camera in the place caught it. But Snelgrove killed that rally for us, sure as hell."

"And he's behind the plate tomorrow night."

Bayly nodded sadly. "Yeah. His umpiring crew's working the series and that's four games of hell for me. A lot of the players are on edge. This series could turn the season around for us. And winning the first game, man, that's key. But I swear Snelgrove'll hurt our chances."

"Perhaps," Henderson said, "and then again…" He let the sentence hang and gave Bayly one of his bright-eyed smiles.

Bayly took the cue and didn't pursue it further. After a moment's silence, he asked, "Why did you come to me about the bracelet?"

Henderson rubbed a thin hand over his smooth pointed jaw. "It's very simple really. I love baseball, have for years. And I admire you as a player. As a child I couldn't play, not well at all. And I'd sit and watch my brothers and the other children running and throwing and hitting and catching. There was something about the game which captivated me. I'd watch every game that came on television. My favourite was Willie Mays, then. I think one always needs a favourite player, like an icon. Over the years, I've had other favourites. They change as careers end and new eras begin. For the past four years, you've been my favourite. Watching you play baseball is almost a religious experience for me. The mighty rip as your bat slices the air is thrilling for me. It's more exciting for me to watch you swing and miss than it is to watch any other player hit a grand slam."

Bayly wasn't sure whether to be insulted or flattered but he didn't say anything. He just kept his eyes on Henderson, whose face was now flushed and whose hands enacted every scene.

"The way you cover the field, the way you run the bases, the way your uniform gets dirty even on artificial turf. There's something magnetic there for me. And when I watched you suffering through that terrible slump, when I heard how the home fans, those fickle, awful people, turned on you, booed you, I knew I had to do something. I knew there was a solution." He paused and looked very proud. "And I was happy to have found it."

"I never did thank you for that, did I?"

"Oh yes. Every time you swing the bat you do." He stood and picked up his briefcase. "I hope to see you again soon, Mr. Bayly."

"Call me Jack."

Henderson's gratitude was so childlike that Bayly felt embarrassed for him. "Thank you, Jack," he said and left the bar.

⌇

Everybody but Bayly was surprised when Buck Snelgrove didn't show up the next day. None of the other umpires knew where he was. He'd left his hotel to go to the stadium and that was the last anyone had seen of him. The other three men in the crew worked the first game. The day after, a replacement was flown in and he stayed for the rest of the series. It wasn't until the fifth inning of the fourth game that Snelgrove was found wandering shoeless through a suburban industrial park. He was unwashed and unshaven and he reported that he'd been forced into a car at gunpoint and blindfolded by somebody wearing a rubber Dracula mask and an old San Francisco Giants cap. He'd been taken somewhere, he'd no idea where exactly, and held there for three days. He'd been well fed, but the kidnapper had said nothing to him. A couple of hand written notes, which the kidnapper immediately destroyed, said he was being held until Sunday afternoon and then he would be released unharmed. "The guy even put the ball games on the radio for me," Snelgrove said with amazement.

After the third inning of that day's game, Snelgrove was blindfolded again, taken to the industrial park, and let off, without his shoes, warned not to take off the blindfold until he counted to one thousand.

Bayly's team swept the weekend series. The opponents filed a protest. And the Commissioner of Baseball launched an investigation. But, in the end, nothing could be proved.

After the Sunday game, Bayly came out of the players' entrance to a horde of autograph seekers. Among them, waiting patiently for his turn, was Henderson.

"Could I have your autograph, please, Mr. Bayly? It's for my son. He's your biggest fan. Could you make it, To Mikey?"

Bayly went along with the charade, but as he wrote his name on the scrap of paper, Henderson whispered, "Great series, Jack."

Without looking up, Bayly said, "Kidnapping's against the law, ain't it?"

"I won't tell if you won't." Then, taking the autograph, he said "Thanks, Mr. Bayly," and vanished into the sea of people.

∽

"I know what your trouble is," Henderson said.

"How did you get my number?" Bayly asked. He was in a foul mood, the latest legal papers from his wife spread all over the kitchen table of his lakeside condo. His wife's settlement demands had gone up to include a share of all Bayly's playing bonuses. And the only calls he was expecting were from his lawyer and from Janine, the woman he'd been seeing regularly for a year and the one his wife was claiming was co-respondent in the divorce proceedings.

"It's easier than you think," Henderson answered.

Bayly took a deep breath. After all, Henderson had bailed him out twice. And Bayly had a fat World Series ring on his finger that way back at the All-Star Break he never figured he'd see. He guessed he owed the guy a little civility. "So you know what my trouble is this time, do you?" Bayly asked.

"Yes, Jack. It's woman trouble, isn't it?"

Bayly laughed. "If I didn't know better, I'd figure you had my phone tapped and a spy satellite hanging around outside my bedroom window."

Henderson joined in with a soft chuckle. "Oh, it's not quite like that, Jack. But I have the root of your problem right here. And I have the solution." Bayly could imagine Henderson patting that fat black briefcase and then tapping a finger against his high temple.

"I sure appreciate everything you've done for me in the past, buddy. But I don't think you can help me now."

"You'd be surprised, Jack. After all, you're my favourite. And I hate to see you suffer."

"I appreciate your concern, but…"

"I'll be in touch soon, Jack."

Bayly listened to the phone go dead and then cradled the receiver. He felt uneasy but didn't know why. He spent another half hour going over the papers. Then he was going to meet his lawyer and go for a showdown with his wife and hers.

He dressed in a suit, something he hated but which lawyers always seemed to demand. Then he headed downstairs. Traffic was good and he was early so he decided to make one quick stop. Just for a little boost of courage.

He pulled up in front of Janine's duplex and walked briskly up to the door, letting himself in. She lived on a busy street that mixed residential houses with small shops and a restaurant or two. From the window of the café across the street you could get a good view of Janine's front door. Several patrons could see Jack Bayly go into the building and then re-emerge, his body contorted in grief, his cries of anguish audible even inside the restaurant.

"Jeez," one of the customers said, the cappuccino stopped halfway to his lips," I wonder what his trouble is."

The small, curly haired, bright eyed man at the next table gave a puzzled frown. "I haven't the slightest idea," he said.

Bush Fever

They said the hammer went into his chest like a runaway train. Snapping the ribs and crushing the heart.

His death had been quick, they said, but it had also been painful. Lying gasping in the mud with the hammer sticking out from under him like a withered limb. The nearest doctor an hour away. The nearest hospital three.

He and Marco worked noon till midnight, and Blake and I came on for the graveyard shift. It was Marco who was swinging the hammer, smashing it on the head of a length of pipe that Tom held steady against the jammed piston, when Marco's foot slipped in the slick mud that spilled from the platform, and his massive arms and shoulders drove the hammer into Tom's body.

∽

The truck pitched and shuddered along the rutted road, headlights darting wildly into the darkness as if desperately seeking shelter. Blake always took the road too fast and it slammed me against the door so the handle dug into my side and then tossed me back against Blake so his elbow made it equal. In the distance, the rig stood bathed in light and reminded me, as it had the first time, of something dropped down from outer space into Alberta's vast and empty north.

As soon as we climbed out of the truck we knew something was wrong. There wasn't the usual activity. We climbed the storey to the drilling platform but there was no one in sight.

Climbing down again, we found them in the pump house. Tom was already dead by the time we got there, covered up with the geologist's coat. Marco sat at the other end of the small space, hands on his knees, empty-eyed.

"Is he dead?" Blake asked, although it seemed pretty obvious to me. Brady, the geologist, nodded and Blake took off his hard hat. "Jesus," he said.

I went over to Marco, whose eyes bored sightlessly into the night. "Christ, Marco. Can I get you something?"

"I slipped," he said, not looking at me. He was covered in mud. "He's dead." I wasn't clear whether he was asking or telling me. But I told him yes and left him in his shock.

The ambulance came soon after. The driver saying it was just as well Tom was dead because, it he hadn't been, the ride to the hospital would have finished him off with a lot more suffering than he'd probably felt.

Tom's body, the ambulance and the local Mounties were gone by four in the morning. The cops took Marco for questioning, but Blake said it was just a formality. Blake watched as their taillights disappeared over the first rise of land, then Brady came up to us. "Let's go," he said.

"Whatcha mean?" I asked.

Blake just shrugged and put his hard hat back on.

The geologist looked at me like I was an idiot. "Let's get this drill operational."

"We had a man get stove in here, Brady," I said. "You expect us to work on like he got a hangnail or something?"

"We're close," Brady said. "And the sooner we get there the sooner we can shut this rig down, move on and start somewhere else." He pointed at Blake. "He's been around long enough to understand that. So get 'er pumping, boys. Now." He turned and walked away.

"Well," I said, "you wanna hold or you wanna swing?"

Blake gave me a grin that took all the cold out of the night and put it in my chest as he reached for the hammer.

We fixed the pump and brought the well in, and they capped it without us seeing Drop One of oil. Each time that happened, even after three months on the rigs, it still flooded me with disappointment. I'd been raised on old movie scenes of men rushing around in a shower of crude as the black gold rained down from gushers spouting a hundred feet in the air. That image had been stuck in my mind when I signed on as a roughneck.

Blake bounced us back to town. Apache Drilling put us up at the local hotel near wherever the mobile rig was located at the time and paid for our room, breakfast and dinner. That was about all we had time for, working twelve-hour shifts twenty-one days straight and then getting four days off.

The hotel room had a bed, chair, rickety table and wallpaper with historic oil wells on it. The bathroom was shared by the hall and, since most of us were roughnecks, the ring was permanent and black as crude. If they'd been smart they'd've enamelled the fixtures black.

I scrubbed the grime off as best I could and met Blake in the saloon for a beer. It was the first time he wanted to talk about what happened.

"Bush fever," he said and sucked the foam off his fourth draft. "It gets to you sometime when you're out there too long. You can see it in the eyes."

"See what?"

"Being alone in the middle of nowhere with that drill working and working, and you a slave to it. It reaches inside you after awhile. And your mind just goes away every now and then."

I tried to remember what I'd seen in Marco's eyes on the rig but I wasn't sure it looked like what Blake was describing or not. "Is that what happened to Marco?"

Blake swished a mouthful of beer around and thought about this for a moment, then swallowed. "Naw. He just slipped." He laughed.

"Hell, couple times up there I nearly lost my grip and took your head with me."

It somehow didn't strike me funny.

Next morning, the desk clerk at the hotel called me as I went down to breakfast. "You know that guy got killed yesterday? What should I do with his stuff?"

"What stuff?"

"We hadda clean out his room. Got a bag full of personal stuff here, and I wanna know what I should do with it."

"How the hell should I know? Didn't somebody from the company call you?"

"Nope." He held the brown grocery bag toward me with both hands. "You worked with him, and I got no address to send it, so if you don't take it I'll toss it."

I took it. Tom wasn't leaving much of a legacy. There was a wind-up watch that didn't wind, a ring of unidentified keys, some socks and underwear and a flannel shirt that was more holes than fabric. There was no cash, of course, and I wondered who I'd see wearing the rest of his clothes and a pair of western boots I recalled him wearing in the saloon a night or two. At the bottom of the bag, there were photographs of two women. One of them I recognized. On the back it said simply, "Sarah" and "15".

That could have been her age, but I doubted it. There was only one hotel in town so I climbed the stairs to the next floor and found room 15. The door was ajar. Through the gap I could see her packing clothes in a well-travelled trunk. She turned towards me when I pushed the half open door wide.

"Sarah?" I said.

She gave me a long steady look, frozen in the act of folding a nightgown that would have been totally useless in the face of a northern Alberta winter. "I've seen you around," she said.

"My name's Cole. I worked the rig with Tom. Well, we worked different shifts, but the same rig."

She went back to folding. "Funny choice of name for a guy working an oil rig."

It wasn't the first time that had been pointed out. She placed a dull patterned dress on top of the negligee. "Were you there when Tom was killed?"

"You know about it, then?"

"Place this size, word gets around fast, Cole." She put a pair of scuffed leather shoes and some patched jeans on top of everything else and closed the lid. It was too full and the latches stayed at least two inches apart.

"Is there anything I can do?" I asked.

"Help me get this closed."

I walked around the trunk and sat on it next to her. Our combined weight forced the lid down and I reached first between my legs and then between hers to snap the latches shut. She touched my knee.

"Are you okay?" I asked her.

She looked puzzled for a minute, then she laughed. "You think Tom and I were lovers."

It was my turn to be puzzled. "Weren't you?"

She shook her head. "No. Marco and I had been, but never Tom."

"Marco?"

"Don't look so surprised. Marco is an attractive man in his own way. He's a few years older than me, but so what? After I broke it off, Tom was ready to step in, if I'd let him. He was a few years younger than me. What difference does it make?"

It didn't, and I said so. "Did Marco think you and Tom were lovers?"

She shrugged. "I know Blake joked about it a few times to Marco in the saloon, but I hardly knew what Marco was thinking even when we were together. Your guess is as good as mine. What difference does it make?" she asked again. "Anyway," she continued, "Tom had nothing to do with me leaving Marco."

"Did Marco know that?"

"I don't think he killed Tom on purpose, if that's what you mean." She stood. "Anyway, I've got a bus. Help me down with this."

The bus stop was outside a five and dime that had a lunch counter running the length of it. Sarah perched on a stool at the end near the window so she could see the bus before it pulled up. I set the trunk on its end next to her. "Can I buy you a coffee?" I asked.

She shrugged. The coffee was not worth drinking, so the mugs stood barely touched in front of us until they went cold. We didn't say anything until the bus arrived ten minutes later. I picked up the trunk again and half dragged it outside.

She bought a ticket from the driver, and he tucked the trunk in the luggage compartment.

"I'm sorry about Tom," I said, as she prepared to board.

She shook her head. "Don't tell that to me. It doesn't matter. His mother is the one you should tell."

I got the name and address of Tom's mother from the head office of Apache Drilling. In case of accidents such as Tom's they always made you put next-of-kin down on the hiring documents. When I asked the girl on the other end of the line for information she didn't even ask why I wanted to know. That made me feel a little uneasy, as if things like this happened all too often.

Tom's mother lived in a small apartment above a convenience store in Edmonton. I rode the bus down three hours with Tom's few possessions in a mended duffel bag on the rack above my head. It slid back and forth as the bus climbed up and down through the foothills.

For some reason, I figured Tom's mother would know about his death. In retrospect, given the way Apache operated, there was no reason why I should have made that assumption. After all, no one else had come forward to claim his things.

As soon as I knocked on the door and she opened it and peered out above the chain I could tell she didn't know. "Yes?" she asked, brushing a wisp of hair back off her forehead.

"My name's Cole. I worked with Tom."

The door closed, the chain dropped, and the door opened again. "What happened?" She wore a snug pair of faded men's jeans and a plaid work shirt that fit her loosely. She must have been very young when Tom was born, for she looked not much older than Sarah.

"It was an accident. On the rig."

She nodded as if she had expected this and stood back to wave me into the apartment. "Please sit down."

Again, she brushed the hair back from her face. It was ginger and streaked lightly with grey, giving her the colouring of a tabby. She had freckles, too, which formed a girlish cluster about her nose. "Coffee? Or a beer?"

Like Sarah, she was calm where I had anticipated hysterics. The death of a son always seemed to me something any parent would be distraught over. As if reading my thoughts, she handed me a beer and said, "I'll cry when you leave, but not until I know what happened."

I explained to her, as simply as possible, how the drill pipe fills with mud as it skewers deeper and deeper and how the pump clears that mud out as steadily as it comes in. If the pump's piston jams in the cylinder, drilling has to stop. And the fastest way to fix things is for one man to hold a length of steel pipe against the jammed piston head and another to hit the pipe as hard as he can with a sledge hammer, jarring the piston loose again.

As I told her she watched my face intently as if she could see the words coming out and scrutinize them for signs that they lied. In the end, when she saw that they didn't, she slumped back in her chair. "Oh, Tommy," she whispered.

"I brought you his things."

"Thank you." She made no motion to take them from me so I set them gently on the coffee table.

"He was my only child," she said then. "He would have been about your age, and he always wanted to work on the oil rigs. I didn't want that, though. I wanted something better, but there comes a time when what your child wants matters more than what you want, and I couldn't stop him. His father worked on the rigs, you see.

"I was fifteen when Tommy was born. His father was two years older. We ran away and lied about our ages and got married in Minneapolis. I never doubted that he loved me, but I wanted my son to have a better life, and when Tommy was born I had to choose, you see. I had to choose between my husband and my son. And I chose to take Tommy away from the oil fields. And away from his father.

"He was very angry. I suppose that's understandable. He blamed the boy for coming between us. I suppose that's understandable, too. I tried to stay in touch. I sent pictures and letters talking about Tommy, hoping his father would change. I never heard anything back but I never stopped writing until a couple of years ago when the letters and pictures started coming back Address Unknown. I don't even know if he ever got any of them at all.

"Tommy never knew his father, you see. That's why he wanted to work the oil fields. So he could find some sense of the man his father was." She gazed at me with such intensity that I had to look away.

"Would you like to see him?" she asked, and went to an old sideboard in the dining room and took out a photo album. It fell open, as if by an invisible hand, and she pointed to a picture of a darkly handsome young man who did not smile. It was faded and about twenty years old, but the face was unmistakable.

I must have stared at it for a long time because she said to me, "Is anything wrong?"

"Did Tom ever see that photo?"

She smiled a sweet, sad smile. "I never showed it to him," she said.

∽

Blake was sitting in the same spot in the saloon when I got back. There was a half empty draft glass in front of him, and for all I knew he might never have moved.

"Where you been?" he asked.

"Went looking for Tom's mother." I sat down.

"Find her?"

"Yes." The waitress brought me two drafts as a reflex. "Sarah said you joked with Marco that she'd left him for Tom."

"A time or two, I guess." He signalled for more beer.

"How did Marco take it?"

Blake smiled. "He got real steamed. I've known him a long while, but I don't think I ever seen him so heated up."

"It must be tough," I said. "A lonely man thinking he'd lost his woman to a guy young enough to be his son. That'd work on your mind like bush fever, wouldn't you think?"

Blake just shrugged and I changed the subject. "By the way," I asked, "before he died, did you tell Tom you were his father?"

Blake's glass stopped before it reached his lips. "I don't know what the hell you're talking about," he said quietly. "But one thing I do know, me and Marco worked these rigs years together. We fixed them pumps maybe thirty times. Maybe forty." He flicked the edge of his glass with a fingernail and it made a soft ping. "And Marco always put that sledge right where he wanted."

Whistling Past the Graveyard

W hen MacDonald woke up in the morning the tune was already running through his head. He couldn't think of what it was called, he had no idea why it was there, and he couldn't make it go away. He found himself whistling it, loudly and off-key, and that just made his hangover worse.

He rolled slowly out of bed. Melanie must have left while he was still asleep. He'd got home from the airport about eight o'clock the night before and she'd met him a couple of hours later at his house. *Their* house, he corrected himself with a smile. The wedding was still two months off but he'd insisted on putting it in both their names as soon as the engagement was announced. He'd asked her to move in with him, too, but she didn't want to do that until the wedding. They'd celebrated his return from Vancouver with a bottle of Scotch, but it hit him hard and he'd faded early.

"Damn," he said to himself as he shuffled around the kitchen with a glass of juice in one hand and a coffee in the other. He tried to concentrate on something other than the song, but as the hangover began to fade, the tune grew stronger. This thing is going to bug me all day, he thought as he climbed, whistling, into the shower.

He whistled the tune as he read the paper and dressed. Never the whole thing, just a few bars of it here and there. Random snatches of the verses and the chorus all jumbled up together.

111

Before leaving his house for work, he searched quickly through his small collection of albums, hoping something would twig, but that didn't help. What little he had was jazz and classical.

Driving downtown, he flipped from station to station, from Top Forty to country to MOR, hoping to discover that it was a current hit he'd overheard somewhere, maybe something he'd heard through the headphones on the plane the night before. But nothing turned up.

After a while he just tried listening to himself to figure out what kind of tune it was, as if that might provide a clue. For a while, he was convinced it was a show tune. Something by Sondheim, he was almost certain. Then it began to feel more like a swing number with lots of horns, then a bluesier thing. That's when he realized he was extemporizing, making up his own arrangements as he went along. Changing the tune, stretching it out, seeing where he could take it.

Jeez, he thought, this thing's turning me into a regular Nelson Riddle. He decided the best thing was just to try to forget about it and eventually the answer would come.

MacDonald worked in a high rise downtown. His office was on the eighth floor, with a view of the lake. He whistled in the elevator, through the reception area, and into his office. He slipped off his jacket and hung it on the back of the door and was just settling in behind his desk when his secretary popped her head in the door. "Welcome back," she said with a smile. "How was the trip?"

"Strictly business," he told her.

"Condemned to be married, he remained blade straight to the end," she said with a laugh. "Don't forget the meeting at ten."

"I'll be there," he said, then he stopped her before she slipped away. She was young, funky, had the sides of her head shaved, and he knew she was dating a guy who played something electronic in a local band. "Patty," he said, "does this tune mean anything to you?" He whistled several bars, but his tunelessness made it incomprehensible.

Patty listened politely, then shook her head, said, "Ten o'clock. Main boardroom. Don't give up your day job," and left.

MacDonald settled down to the work that had accumulated in the week he'd been gone. Patty stuck her head in the door again a short time later. "It's five after ten," she said. "They're waiting. And don't whistle like that in the meeting. Jacobs has absolutely no appreciation for music."

The meeting helped take MacDonald's mind off the music, but when it broke up at noon, the tune popped right back. It's like being possessed, he thought with a chuckle. Maybe I need an exorcist. Instead, he went to a music store.

He found the least harassed-looking clerk and asked him the obvious question. Then he tried whistling the tune as close to its original form as he could. When he had finished, the clerk just stared at him and didn't say anything.

"Thank you anyway," MacDonald said and started towards the door.

"Wait," the clerk called after him. "Er, wait a second. I'm not sure if I know, but someone else might." He moved closer to MacDonald and leaned in and stared hard as if he were trying to count freckles. "Why don't you leave me your name, address, and phone number and we'll get in touch with you as soon as we know."

MacDonald felt uneasy. He didn't like the intensity with which the man was looking at him. Something felt very wrong. MacDonald decided not to wait. "Thanks," he said, "but it isn't that important."

He left the store quickly and walked a block and a half down the street and turned the corner before he stopped and leaned against the wall. He realized he was out of breath and his hands were shaking.

All afternoon he tried not to whistle or hum the tune. He tried to keep it out of his mind completely. But no matter how deeply he buried himself in his ledgers and balance sheets, it kept burrowing to the surface like a mole. He was happier than usual when five o'clock dragged around and he put on his suit jacket and slipped out the door. He took the stairs down instead of the elevator, not wanting to catch himself whistling in a crowd.

He got in his car and drove to Melanie's apartment, hoping she would recognize the tune.

113

Melanie was waiting for him with a glass of wine. He took it and drank before he kissed her. "What's wrong?" she asked immediately.

MacDonald dropped onto the sofa. "It's weird," he said. "This tune has been going through my head all day and I can't shake it. I can't figure out what it is. And when I asked a guy in a record store I got the strangest reaction."

"Try me," Melanie said, curling up on the sofa next to him.

A few bars into the tune, Melanie started to smile.

MacDonald's hopes rose. "You know it?"

She shook her head. "I don't even think the guy who wrote it would recognize it. Your whistling stinks. Try again."

He whistled a few more bars, then trailed off discordantly. "Well?"

Melanie had stopped smiling and was looking at him just as strangely as the clerk in the record store.

"What?" he asked.

"What time is it?" she asked, jumping off the sofa and glancing at her watch. "Six ten. Good." She crossed the room and snapped on the television.

"You're telling me it's the theme from a sitcom or something?" He'd hoped for something less banal.

"Sh. Watch."

MacDonald recognized a familiar local news announcer gazing balefully at the camera as he relayed some unsettling financial news. Behind his head, a jagged line rose and fell, creating what looked like an unfortunate set of horns. MacDonald wondered if the director was sleeping with the announcer's wife and this was his little joke. But that thought left him quickly when the next item came up. The graphic changed to a picture of a blood-covered knife.

MacDonald's skin prickled as he listened. "There was another in the string of killings that have terrorized area residents over the past five weeks. Last night's victim was twenty-three-year-old student Susan Larraby. Her body was found in a secluded area by joggers early this morning. Police remain baffled by the killings, now four since the first victim, nineteen-year-old Debbie Deneau, was found more than

114

five weeks ago. The only significant clue remains the mysterious whistling, which three different witnesses claim to have heard near three of the murder sites. None of the witnesses could identify the tune, but all three did say the whistling was badly off-key."

"Jesus," he said, staring at the screen long after Melanie had switched it off. "You don't think that just because I can't carry a tune ..."

"Look," she cut him off, "we know you're no killer." But when MacDonald looked at her he wondered if he saw a flicker of doubt in her eyes.

"No," he said, "I'm not. The only thing I killed last night was a bottle." He hoped he sounded convincing.

"But the way people are feeling right now, just the act of whistling could cause you a lot of trouble."

MacDonald had never been one for the news. He read the sports page and the business press at work, and he enjoyed longer pieces in magazines, but he never read the paper at home. He paid little attention to hard news stories. Global affairs were beyond him and local news bored him. But now he had to know more. "Do you have the papers for the last few weeks?" he asked.

Melanie nodded. "The last couple. A bunch I'm keeping for packing and the rest I just bundled up for recycling. Come on, we'll dig them out."

In two minutes Melanie's living-room floor was littered with newspapers and MacDonald had every line about the rash of killings clutched in his ink-stained hands. He went back to the sofa while Melanie rebundled the papers and pored over the reports, reading everything. The screaming headlines ranged from the responsible, "Slayer Claims Fourth Victim," to the hysterical, "Killer Whistles While He Works." The sidebars, which featured interviews with grieving friends and family, MacDonald found intensely distasteful, and he reminded himself why he had stopped reading the paper in the first place.

The facts varied little from victim to victim. Four young women, the youngest nineteen, the eldest twenty-eight, all stabbed to death with what appeared to be the same weapon. All the bodies were found in or near small clumps of bushes. None had been sexually molested. None had been robbed. So far, any forensic evidence had yielded nothing significant; at least, nothing the police were talking about. But there was the music. The unidentifiable tune three witnesses all claimed to have heard within fifteen minutes and five hundred yards of three different murder sites.

MacDonald read it all twice. Then he sat silently for a long time trying to convince himself that he didn't slip into some distant recess of his soul and do things that sickened him while Melanie slept. He spent the evening pacing the floor without talking. Three times he found himself whistling and he cut it off with a curse, wondering how long he'd been doing it. Melanie left him alone, making sure he knew she was there if he wanted to talk but not trying to initiate it. At eleven o'clock, he went to the television set and turned it on. Melanie settled on the couch beside him and placed a hand lightly on his knee. He covered it with his own and they watched in silence.

Ten minutes into the newscast, they repeated the story from earlier in the day. A few details had been added, all but one insignificant. This report added the news that an unidentified man had asked a local record-store clerk to identify a tune he was whistling. The clerk couldn't, but felt the man's behavior was so peculiar he called the police. Then the screen was filled with a frighteningly accurate computer-generated likeness of MacDonald.

The phone rang ten minutes later, rupturing the silence in the room. They exchanged glances and Melanie whispered, "What should we do?" as if the person on the other end of the line could hear her. MacDonald just nodded and she picked up the phone. "Hello?" she said. MacDonald watched the tension melt from her face and heard her laugh with relief and she held the phone out to him. "It's Pike," she said.

MacDonald took the phone and before he could say anything, Pike was talking. "They got you pegged pretty good there, pal. Although the picture was a little too good-looking to be spot on. What the hell happened?"

MacDonald started to tell him, then said, "I don't want to talk about it on the phone. I don't know what the hell to do."

"Sit tight. Don't answer the phone. Don't answer the door or anything. I'm on my way over. I'll be there in half an hour." And he hung up.

MacDonald tried to sit tight, but found he couldn't sit at all. Melanie watched him pace a circuit around the small apartment, from room to room in a tireless parade Twenty minutes later he was in the kitchen getting a drink when Pike rapped on the door with a jaunty shave-and-a-haircut rhythm and Melanie heard the smash of a glass and MacDonald swearing sharply.

Melanie opened the door and Pike breezed through, glancing a kiss off her cheek and pulling off his coat as he moved.

The three of them had been friends ever since Pike had come to work in the office next to MacDonald's. He'd left again eight months later; changing jobs was as habitual with him as changing girlfriends, but he and MacDonald had stayed in close touch. They met two or three times a month for lunch, and he was a frequent dinner guest at both MacDonald's house and Melanie's apartment. Often, they would go to Pike's place. It was a small, one-bedroom apartment which Pike frequently claimed he was chained to, likely unable ever to afford a house at Toronto prices. "Where's the villain?" he asked as Melanie closed and locked the door.

Melanie jerked her head towards the kitchen and Pike walked over and saw MacDonald on his knees, sweeping shards of glass into a battered metal dustpan. "I'm surprised they let you handle anything sharp," Pike said with a laugh.

"This isn't funny." MacDonald's edginess made the words snap out more harshly than he'd intended. "Sorry," he added as he dumped the glass into the garbage.

"I understand. No problem. Because of some weird coincidence you could be in big trouble. That'd put me on edge, for sure. But we'll sort it out. We know you're not the guy. It'll be easy enough to prove. We'll just plot out your life for the last five weeks." He opened the fridge door and peered in. "You want a drink?"

MacDonald nodded. "I didn't get much of my last one."

"Wine, beer?"

MacDonald's stomach turned over. "Just juice."

Pike poured it out and twisted open a beer for himself and continued. "We write down every move you made for the whole time, as much as you can remember. Then we retrace the steps. We're bound to come up against people that remember you, who can put you certain places at the times that prove you couldn't have killed anybody."

"But I didn't kill anybody."

Pike put a hand on his chest. "I know that. You know that. She knows that. But the cops aren't as wise as us."

"Maybe not, but they sure aren't stupid, and now that they've got my picture on network TV I expect to see a couple of uniforms at my door any minute. And they won't be selling raffle tickets for the Widows' and Orphans' Fund."

"Hey, hey, calm down. It's eleven thirty at night. Most of the people you know won't have seen that at all. The rest of them won't believe it was you. How long was it on the screen? Four, five seconds? Tomorrow, when it's in the paper, that's when you got trouble."

"This is supposed to make me calm down?"

Pike shrugged and sipped his beer. "Look, what it means is we've got until business opens tomorrow to figure out a plan. First, tell me all about how they got your picture."

When MacDonald was finished, Pike whistled softly. "Jeez, what a fluke. What are the odds that some guy selling records is going to put that together and call the cops? Just your luck you had to run into an upstanding citizen."

"Fluke or not, it happened, and now my face is out there for everybody to see. How far do you think we'll get without my being recognized?"

Pike waved his hand in dismissal. "We'll throw a disguise on you. A hat and some glasses and nobody'll know you from Adam. All the time the cops run hunts for people a lot less ordinary looking than you with their faces plastered all over the place and nobody ever turns them in. People don't make the connection between what a mocked-up picture looks like on an over-inked newspaper page and somebody in the flesh. Besides, we don't need five weeks. We can retrace your steps, what we need to, in a day." He turned to Melanie. "We'll need a few sheets of paper and a pen." He sat on the sofa. "Oh, and another beer."

For the next two hours they sat huddled around the coffee table as Pike jotted down details from the last month and a half of MacDonald's life. From the moment he woke up on the morning of the first murder until Melanie arrived at his house the evening before. There were gaps, of course, and a lot of dates and times were sketchy, but Pike made note of places and people who might have some reason for remembering MacDonald, no matter how obscure. The waiter he undertipped at lunch one day and the bookstore clerk he chatted with briefly another. In the end it covered four sheets of paper in Pike's cramped, illegible hand. MacDonald looked at it in dismay. "I hope you can read that," he said.

Pike looked at it, then nodded. "Maybe I'll clean it up a little."

While Pike transcribed parts of the list, MacDonald looked at the newspaper again. He opened to an article that featured pictures of all the victims. He looked carefully at the row of faces, feeling a mixture of sadness at their fate and anger that he was being blamed. Each picture was square, cut to exactly the same dimensions. One was a graduation photo. One was obviously clipped from a family portrait, an anonymous shoulder protruding into the frame. Another looked like a photo from the kind of vending machines you find in bowling alleys, shopping malls, and bus stations.

In each case he saw a young, smiling face framed by dark hair hanging to the shoulders and beyond and parted in the middle. He noticed that each of them had the same eyebrows, long, dark, and arching. Each woman had a similar nose and chin and the same broad forehead. Each woman, he realized with growing horror, could have been mistaken for Melanie.

He tossed the paper to the floor and Melanie and Pike turned to look at him. "What's the matter?" Melanie asked.

"You look like you've seen a ghost," Pike said.

"Maybe four of them," MacDonald said. "I need that drink now."

He walked across the room and rattled the bottles in the liquor cabinet, looking for the Scotch. Finding it, he poured a few ounces into a glass and swallowed half. He took the glass back to his seat, leaving the bottle uncorked on the liquor cabinet.

Pike had picked up the paper and was looking at the pictures. "Mel," he said, "look at this."

As she looked, she shook her head. "Mac...," she started to say, then let it hang.

Pike broke the silence. "Let's start by thinking. The cops say all these women were killed by the same guy, so all we have to do is cook up an alibi for you for one of the killings and you'll be clear."

MacDonald nodded. That made sense to him. If only he could remember what he'd done when. As with most people, dates tended to fade and run together in his memory, unless there was a ticket stub or credit card slip or other tangible souvenir to remind him of exactly where he'd been on a given day.

"We'll work backwards," Pike said, "from the last one. They must give time of death or something in the paper." He rustled through the pages, scanning quickly. "Here. She was found at approximately ten twenty. You weren't scheduled to come in until half past. This should do it right there."

MacDonald shook his head. "I took an earlier flight. I even called Melanie from Vancouver. I was in here by seven thirty. Lots of time to get anywhere in the city." He drained his glass and went for a refill.

"What about the one before?"

Melanie turned to the paper this time. "Okay, she was killed some-time between six fifteen, when she was last seen alive, and seven fifty, when the body was found. On Tuesday, the eighteenth."

Pike rubbed his jaw and thought. "The eighteenth?" Pike turned to the notes. "The eighteenth?"

"The library," MacDonald said. "That was the day we took the afternoon off to celebrate my raise and we had that argument about Terry Sawchuck's goals against average, or something stupid like that, and we went to the library to check it out."

"That's it," Pike said, snapping his fingers. "That's it. I'm just sur-prised you remember any of it at all, you were so tanked up, but they'll remember us at the library for sure." He looked at this watch. "Jesus, it's late. I'm gonna go home and catch a few winks. I'll be back here early and we'll wrap this thing up, no problem. You get some sleep, Mac, and we'll see you in the morning." He clapped MacDonald on the shoulder, kissed Melanie on the cheek, and left.

MacDonald tried to sleep but spent most of the night standing at the balcony doors looking out over the city wondering if he would suddenly be seized by the desire to kill. And wondering whether Melanie would be next. He didn't say this to her, didn't say much of anything, and after a while she slipped quietly away and went to bed.

When dawn came through the glass it found MacDonald dozing fitfully on the sofa. Melanie found him there, too.

Pike was back at nine o'clock. He came into the apartment with a newspaper under his arm and a paper shopping bag in his hand. He tossed the bag to MacDonald and handed the paper to Melanie. "Put those on," he said.

MacDonald looked into the bag. "What for?"

"We're going to the library."

"If I go outside, someone'll recognize me."

"If you stay in here, you got no chance to defend yourself. Put on the disguise."

Reluctantly, MacDonald pulled a long coat with a high collar, a hat, and a pair of sunglasses from the bag. He turned up the collar and pulled the hat low over his face. He was about to put on the shades when Melanie said softly, "Oh, my God."

MacDonald looked at her and she handed him the paper. There, on the front page, was another Melanie look-alike and a screaming headline, "Serial Killer Strikes in Vancouver?".

MacDonald was too stunned to react. He just stared at the paper as Pike read over his shoulder. "They just found the body last night, but she'd been missing three days," he said. "It says the knife wounds match the ones on the victims here."

MacDonald started to laugh slightly. "I don't believe this. How the hell am I going to explain this? You may as well call the cops right now. They already think I did it. Now I'm in Vancouver for six lousy days and there's a killing there, too. Maybe I did do it, I don't know."

"Knock it off," Pike said. "Start thinking like that and you're finished. Come on, let's go to the library."

The library was a sprawling one-storey building that sat on one corner of a city block. A row of maples separated the building from the sidewalk, and the rest of the block was taken up by a large park, half wooded and half playground.

MacDonald was slouched in the back seat of Pike's car, his face almost totally hidden behind the hat and glasses. "Wasn't one of the bodies found in a park?" he asked as Pike pulled up in front of the library.

Pike nodded. "Yep."

"This one," Melanie added, her voice a whisper.

"Jesus," MacDonald said as he climbed out of the car.

The library desk was opposite the front doors, with the adult section to the left and children's books to the right. At the back of the adult section was a reading area in which a handful of chairs formed a ring around a low wooden table littered with magazines. Along the outside walls stood several study carrels and the high glass windows looked out over the park. Near the back of the section they could see a librarian taking books from a trolley and reshelving them. A second librarian was doing paperwork behind the counter. Pike approached her and cleared his throat. "Excuse me," he said.

The librarian looked up. She was middle-aged and her eyes were very bright and eager. "May I help you?" she asked in a way that made you not want her to start helping for fear that she might never stop.

"Yes," Pike said. MacDonald winced as he waited to find out what was coming. "I'm wondering if you were on duty on Tuesday evening, the eighteenth?"

"Why do you ask? Are you from the police?"

MacDonald wanted to scream and run but found his legs would not move. Pike was unperturbed. "Why, you haven't been writing in the books, have you, or folding back the corners of the pages?" He gave her his warmest smile and she joined in on the joke with a smile of her own. "No," Pike went on, "we're not police. Far from it. It's just that my friend was in here that night and he may have left something behind."

The librarian peered carefully at MacDonald, who was thankful he hadn't taken off his glasses. "What did he leave?" she asked, as if MacDonald wasn't there at all, although she was still staring right at him.

"Some notes. Research. We just wonder if anyone here found them, or if you even remember seeing him in here."

"Well, I'm pretty good with faces, but I can't be sure unless he takes those sunglasses off."

Pike nudged MacDonald. "Take 'em off."

MacDonald looked at Melanie for help but she just nodded. He slipped off the glasses. It felt like he was taking off his clothes on the subway.

"And the hat," the librarian said.

MacDonald complied and the librarian peered at him for a long time. Then her eyes lit up even more. "Yes," she said, "of course. He was here and I had to ask him to be quiet. It was Tuesday night. I must say, he seemed a little bit tipsy."

Pike nodded. "One of his stocks went way up. He made a killing and he was celebrating. You're sure it was the eighteenth?"

She looked mildly offended. "Of course I'm sure. I remember because of the whistling."

"Whistling?" Pike asked.

MacDonald's lungs felt like they were being squeezed.

"Yes. It was disturbing some people. You know, we do try to maintain an atmosphere conducive to study."

"Of course," Pike said, with great understanding. "Was the whistling that loud?"

"Not so much loud as" - she hunted for the right word - "atonal. Off-key." A touch of mist clouded her eyes as she added, "The way my late husband used to whistle." Then her eyes settled on Melanie. "You were with him, too," she said firmly. "And so, now that I think of it, were you." She settled her gaze on Pike. "But then when we were closing we found this one alone, sleeping in one of the carrels. It took forever to wake him up and —"

"What time was that?" Pike interrupted.

"Closing time. Eight thirty."

"You're sure it was him?"

"Absolutely. But I don't remember any notes," she said. "Except the whistling. Musical notes." Pike smiled politely and they left the library.

Back in the car, safely behind his glasses and drooping hat, MacDonald said, "So what does that all mean?"

"What it means, buddy, is that you have an alibi for one of the killings. And, since all the killings were done by the same person, that puts you in the clear."

Melanie turned in her seat to smile at MacDonald. "This calls for a celebration," she said.

The roast was cooking at 350 degrees and Pike was in the kitchen washing vegetables as Melanie set the table and MacDonald sat on the sofa, sipping a glass of wine. They'd gone back to Pike's place, trying to buy a little extra time before the police arrived. MacDonald wasn't sure why, but he'd stopped worrying about that happening. He was sure they would soon enough, but it didn't bother him too much. Knowing he had even a scrap of an alibi helped somewhat, but mostly it was just that he felt resigned, and it was less painful to accept the inevitable than to rail against it.

He watched Melanie as she laid out the place settings. He noticed she was using all the crystal and china, setting the forks on the cloth napkins and spoons and steak knives down just as silently. She put out water in a cut-glass pitcher and opened a fine Merlot and poured it with a soft gurgling into a Waterford decanter.

Satisfied, she said, "I'm going downstairs to get the paper. I'll be back in a few minutes." She went out and pulled the door shut behind her. MacDonald noticed that it didn't click all the way to and he got up and walked across to close it. As he passed the kitchen he noticed that Pike (as he always did, MacDonald realized) was whistling to himself as he cooked. MacDonald recognized a snatch of *Melancholy Baby* and then a larger piece of *The Lady Is a Tramp*. And then he heard something that froze him in his tracks. A song he knew well, one that had long been a favourite of Melanie's. He knew exactly what it was but something in him had to make sure. He asked, trying to keep his voice casual, "What's that song, Pike?"

"Huh? Oh, *Mac the Knife*. Speaking of knives, can you bring me the one from the table, please?"

"One of the steak knives?" MacDonald asked.

"No, the big carving knife. I need to sharpen it."

It lay to the right of Pike's place at the table, the blade elevated on a knife rest. MacDonald picked it up. "This new?" he asked, telling himself his suspicions were all wrong. "I've never seen it before."

"Yeah," Pike said. "It's only been used a few times. Nice, huh? Feel the balance on it."

MacDonald moved the knife up and down on the palm of his hand. "Feels okay, I guess."

"You bet. Give it a good grip. See how natural it feels in your hand."

MacDonald wrapped his fist around the handle. It felt hard and cold and solid. Then MacDonald turned the knife sideways and ran it across his thumbnail, peeling off a thin layer of tissue. "It seems pretty sharp already," he said.

"Yeah," Pike said. "But I like it to be just so, you know?"

MacDonald stood just outside the kitchen holding the knife, the strange knife he'd never seen before and which felt so good in his hand, and listened to Pike's whistling and it all became clear to him.

"Mac, can I have the knife please?" Pike said.

MacDonald went into the kitchen. "What did you think?" he asked. "That you could pin it on me and she would fall into your arms?"

Pike hadn't been paying attention. "Huh?" he grunted.

"You've always been close with her. Maybe closer than I suspected. You know my house is already half in her name. You know the bank accounts are transferred. You thought if I was arrested she'd turn to you, taking my house with her." MacDonald's voice was flat and calm but his eyes were wide and dilated.

Pike looked at him and at the knife, which was now waving in the air between them, and he held out his hand. "Just give me the knife please, Mac," he said softly, reaching out a rubber-gloved hand from which soap suds dripped steadily.

Of course, MacDonald told himself, gloves. He's wearing gloves, and like a fool I've been blithely smearing the knife with my fingerprints. Incriminating myself as surely as if I'd confessed. The knife that's been used only a few times, to slit a few pale throats. Pike took a step forward, gloved hand still outstretched and MacDonald started to back away, then realized he still held the knife and feinted forward. Pike jerked back, his hands coming up in front of his face abruptly, throwing droplets of water across the room, hitting MacDonald's face like spring rain.

"How could you do it?" MacDonald asked, taking a step forward.

Pike moved back again. "I don't know what you're talking about," he said, his tongue darting out to moisten suddenly dry lips. "Please, just give me the knife."

"So you can use it on me?" MacDonald asked, closing the gap again.

Pike tried a joke, because surely to God, MacDonald was only joking. "I only want to use it on the roast," Pike said.

"How stupid do you think I am?" MacDonald asked, the knife moving in wide sweeping circles, which Pike watched with hypnotized fascination, like a small animal watching the dance of the cobra. Each man took another step into the kitchen and Pike felt his legs press against the small kitchen table. End of the line.

"How could you kill all those women? You knew where I was as well as I did. You killed them near where I'd been. You did it knowing I'd been seen. You whistled that tune, hoping I'd pick it up. You even flew to Vancouver when I was there to make things even more perfect. I know everything you've done, but you won't get away with it. You won't make me your scapegoat."

"It wasn't like that…" Pike started to say, then realized it was useless. Abruptly, he lunged to his left towards the open cutlery drawer. He knew exactly where the steak knives were but his fingers were clumsy in the rubber gloves, and by the time they closed around the handle of one and he swung around to point it at MacDonald, he felt the sharpness of the carving knife as it tore between his ribs. He tried to bring his arm up to defend himself, but it wouldn't respond. Then he felt the bite of the carving knife again, heard somewhere the distant clatter of his own knife hitting the floor, and then watched as the room spun around him as he fell.

MacDonald was kneeling over Pike when the apartment door opened and Melanie came in. "Mac!" she called out.

He tried to answer her but couldn't find his voice. He heard her looking in the bedroom and the bathroom, calling his name. Then he became aware of her standing in the kitchen door. "Oh, my God," she said quietly.

"He killed them," MacDonald heard himself saying. "He killed all of them and he wanted to pin it on me, so I'd be out of the way, so he could have you and the house and the money." He realized that he was sobbing.

"I'd better call the police," Melanie said and went into the living room.

As she punched 911 and waited for a response, MacDonald could hear her whistling to herself. Kneeling beside Pike's body, he couldn't help but notice how off-key she sounded.

The Vampires Next Door

The vampires next door were having a party. It didn't happen often. Generally they were pretty quiet neighbours. Nathan hardly knew they were there half the time. But once every two or three months they'd have friends in and things would get a little livelier.

From the beginning, Nathan wondered what the parties were like. Did vampires dance? If so, what kind of music did they play? Were the conversations intricate and philosophical discussions or shallow and transitory chit chat? Were charades popular? Nathan even tried to envisage what they served as canapés. He already knew how the bar was stocked.

The morning after the second of the vampires' parties, Nathan found an empty plasma bag lying in the hall between the vampires' front door and the incinerator room. It was then around ten in the morning and the empty bag must have been lying there since before dawn, making Nathan wonder how many people had seen it on their way to the elevators but had simply pretended it wasn't there.

Nathan went back into his apartment, put on the rubber gloves he used for washing dishes, and picked up the empty bag. He took it into the incinerator room and dropped it and the gloves down the chute. Then he washed his hands for a long time under very hot water.

The night of the vampires' first party, Nathan had been very nervous. He knew the fear was irrational. After all, the vampires had told him all the things he needed to do in order to stay safe. Still, there he was, living next door to a couple of undead things that survived by drinking human blood. And they were having company. He was terrified.

He tried telling himself it was no different than living next to a couple with any other dietary quirk. Vegetarians perhaps, or Catholics who still ate fish on Friday. Or people who always ate the middle of the Oreo first, or the red Smarties last. He tried thinking that way, but it didn't really help.

The vampires had been very good about preparing Nathan for their first party. Three days before, they came to Nathan's apartment for a visit. They brought a bottle of Bordeaux dated 1837 and they sat on the sofa holding hands. Every once in awhile one or the other would laugh at something that was said and their fangs would peek briefly from behind their burgundy lips, causing Nathan to suppress a shudder.

"We're going to have a party," Bianca told him.

Nathan's jaw dropped. "A party? Like an open house? For the neighbours?" He couldn't help wondering if anyone else in the building knew.

"No, silly," Bianca said. Laughter. Fangs. "For our old friends."

"Friends?"

"Yes," Mikhail told him. "Some friends from uptown. Some friends from other parts of the country. And some friends who just flew in from overseas."

Nathan smiled weakly. "And, boy, are their arms ever tired," he said.

Mikhail looked confused. "Yes," he said in his rumbling tones, "the strain it puts on the muscles here..." He started to indicate areas of the upper arm and shoulder when Bianca laid her hand on Mikhail's wrist and stopped him.

"It's an old joke," she said.

"Oh," Mikhail said, looking embarrassed. Nathan figured he came as close to blushing as a vampire ever could.

"The party will be Friday night," Bianca said.

The thirteenth, Nathan thought. Figures.

"We're expecting a large number of guests. We'll try and be as quiet as possible. The parties seldom become rowdy unless an infiltrator is found. Then things can get out of hand. If you're planning to be home that night, we advise you to take several precautions." Then she described in detail how Nathan could use crosses and garlands of fresh garlic to keep any overly enthusiastic partygoers at bay.

"But I don't take these precautions with you."

"That's because of our arrangement. Unfortunately, our friends aren't all as" - she paused, hunting for the right word - *"avant garde* as we are. If you're careful, the worst that should happen will be the odd annoying phone call. You'd perhaps be best not to answer the phone at all that night."

The next day, Nathan bought several crosses in a variety of sizes from a Christian supply store he found in the Yellow Pages. Then he went to his local grocer and bought all the garlic buds they had. The grocer looked at him oddly as Nathan piled up the fragrant vegetables on the counter.

"I'm making soup," Nathan said.

The grocer nodded. "Thought maybe you were worried about vampires or something," he said. "'Course, you make a soup with this much garlic, you'll keep more'n them suckers away." He laughed, showing wide, uneven teeth.

Nathan smiled back unhappily and walked home with his packages.

As it turned out, the party was one of the most subdued Nathan had ever lived beside. There were some peculiar noises, what he thought was the flapping of leathery wings outside his window, and what sounded like a large dog sniffing loudly at the base of his front door, but for the most part he was not bothered.

At two in the morning his phone did ring, as Bianca had told him it might, and a cold, hypnotic voice said, "Come next door and be the life of the party." But the call was abruptly cut off and Nathan unplugged the phone and sat up on the sofa for the rest of the night.

Nathan hadn't realized at first that his new neighbours were vampires, although it was unusual to have people moving in after midnight. He'd heard them thumping and banging in the halls and he recognized the universal cries of the do-it-yourself mover:

"A little to the left."

"Hangonhangonhangonhangon!"

"Just let me get a better grip."

He went out into the hall to have a look, and that's when he got his first glimpse of Bianca.

Her back was to him, clad entirely in black, with lustrous hair, the blackest Nathan had ever seen, falling almost to her slender waist. She wore snug black designer jeans (Nathan spent a long time trying to read the label) and black leather boots reached up almost to her knees. She was moving backwards toward the open door of the apartment next to Nathan's, and she was struggling with an awkward looking box. As she moved she was giving directions to two men who followed her carrying a large, dark wooden chest, like a long, low sideboard, with ornate brass handles.

They were big, fierce looking men and Nathan hoped they hadn't noticed him looking so longingly at the woman's behind. He stepped forward. "Let me help," he said, grabbing the other end of the awkward box in the woman's arms.

She shot him a look of consternation. Sensing that perhaps she was new to the big city and uneasy about strange men offering assistance in the middle of the night, Nathan said, "I live next door." He pointed to his apartment and smiled at her with such bland innocence that she let him take some of the weight of the box. Nathan's knees buckled and the smile left his face. He'd expected linens or something, but it felt like there was an anvil in there. He struggled forward, expecting any second to feel something in his stomach tear apart.

They brought the box into the living room and set it down, Nathan dropping his end with a grunt and a crash the neighbours below must have loved. The woman set her end down as gently as a mother laying a newborn's head on a pillow. Nathan wondered how many hours she'd spent on a Nautilus machine to be able to do that.

The two men followed them into the apartment and set the sideboard against the dining room wall.

"That's it," the woman said. "That's everything." She turned her gaze to Nathan and his heart swelled. He'd never seen eyes so black and he instantly fell in love. "Thank you, Mr..."

Nathan held out a hand. "Nathan," he said. "Since we're going to be neighbours, just call me Nathan."

"My name is Bianca." She took Nathan's hand. The night outside was edging down toward freezing, and she'd been working without gloves, so her hand was cold. Releasing Nathan's grip, she indicated the two men with her.

"This," she said, pointing to a tall man with heavy shoulders, a handsome face deeply lined by the elements and eyes nearly as dark as her own, "is my husband Mikhail." Mikhail looked at Nathan with penetrating intensity and bowed slightly and briskly. "And this is our friend, Raoul." She drew the second syllable out so that the name sounded like an abbreviated howl. Raoul was, Nathan thought, the hairiest man he'd ever seen, his eyes sandwiched between a thick beard and heavy overhanging eyebrows.

Raoul immediately turned to Mikhail, grunted something, then stalked out of the apartment.

"You must excuse Raoul," Bianca said. "He's a little lacking in the social graces. He's something of a lone wolf."

Nathan nodded. "Well," he said, "I better be going too. If there's anything else you need, I'm right next door."

"Must you go?" Bianca edged closer to him, her tongue moistening her upper lip.

"Won't you stay for a little nightcap?" Mikhail's voice was rich and textured, like a Slavic Richard Burton. "After all we're your new neighbours and you can give us a little taste of life in the building." There was something about the way Mikhail said it, and the way Bianca was rubbing her cold hands over Nathan's chest, that made him nervous.

"That's awfully nice of you," Nathan said, "but I have to work tomorrow, and it's so late..." He began backing toward the door.

"Oh? And what work do you do?" Bianca asked, although it sounded to Nathan like a polite cocktail party question.

"I work at a blood bank," Nathan said. "Testing blood."

Bianca pulled back from Nathan as if she'd been stung. He'd had that reaction before from women who thought his job was disgusting.

He couldn't understand it, really. What he was doing was very important. What with all the horrible bacteria swimming around in the world's blood streams he, and those like him, were all that stood between national health and pandemia. So he wasn't surprised when Bianca drew away. He was surprised when he looked at her face, and then at Mikhail's, and saw a level of interest he'd never witnessed before.

"What exactly do you do," Bianca purred, "with the blood?"

"Well," Nathan confessed, "I don't actually do the testing. But they look for HIV, HBV, HCV, syphilis, you name it, before they store it or ship it out for operations, transfusions, whatever. Naturally, they don't want to keep the bad stuff. That's my job. I'm in charge of disposal. There's a joke around the lab, there's always bad blood between me and everyone else."

Bianca laughed and Mikhail smiled ever so slightly. Then Bianca placed a hand on Nathan's elbow and steered him to the door with a strength that made him increase his estimate of how much time she'd spent in the gym. "But we must let you get some sleep. You have important work. And Mikhail and I have much to discuss about arrangements here in our new home."

The arrangements were made plain to Nathan two days later. Mikhail and Bianca invited him over for a drink and, they said, a chance to get better acquainted. Nathan wasn't entirely comfortable after their peculiar behaviour of the other night, but he found himself curiously unable to refuse.

Nathan sat in a very comfortable arm chair and looked at Mikhail and Bianca on the sofa. "So," he said with a smile, "now it's my turn." He took a sip of the wine they offered him. It had turned, but he tried not to show it. After all, unless the label was a gag, the bottle was over one hundred and fifty years old. "What do you guys do for a living?"

Mikhail and Bianca looked at one another for quite some time. It was obvious to Nathan that they were trying to figure out how to answer, or even if they should. Maybe I shouldn't have asked, he thought. Maybe they do something really weird or gross. Maybe they're worm pickers and that's why you never see them during the day. Maybe they run a phone sex business. He mentally kicked himself. But just as he was about to try to steer the conversation in a new direction, Bianca turned her eyes from Mikhail to him.

"We're vampires," she said simply. Just like that. Flat out and straight faced. Like she was telling the guy at the deli how much smoked meat she wanted.

Nathan stared at her. "Pardon me?"

"We're vampires."

"You know, the undead," Mikhail added, by way of helpful explanation.

Nathan started to laugh. "You guys," he said, slapping his knee with a loud flat sound. "The clothes, the crazy hours. Look, if you don't want to tell me what you do, I understand. Everybody has secrets. It's okay with me."

Bianca shook her head. "We're not kidding, Nathan. We're really vampires."

There was something in her tone that made Nathan stop laughing. He'd heard of people who called themselves vampires. Little groups of fringe dwellers, the kind of wingnuts you found clinging like barnacles to the underside of any big city. People who drank the blood of animals or licked it from small wounds opened in one another's chests and fingertips, late at night, in the glow of dripping candles, often for sexual reasons.

Nathan looked at the thick crimson richness of the wine in his glass and felt queasy. Maybe they were being serious. Maybe they did consider themselves vampires. Maybe they were the kind of lunatics he'd really rather not have living next door, the kind he certainly didn't want to spend the evening with in idle chatter while they sized up which of his veins to open first. He started calculating how far it was to the front door.

Mikhail leaned forward suddenly. "We'll prove it to you," he said brightly.

"That's okay!" Nathan threw up his hands and shrank back. "If you say you're vampires, hey, who am I to argue?" He looked at his watch. "Whoa, where does the time go? I really...I gotta...I..."

Mikhail waved off his objections. "No, no," he said. "We must prove it to you. We sense, very strongly, that you are not sure in here." He touched the middle of his chest. "We will not rest easily if we feel there is any doubt."

Nathan was frantic. "I don't doubt! I don't doubt! Please don't feel you have anything to prove on my account."

"But we will," Mikhail barked. "Look!" Then he and Bianca pulled their lips back in exaggerated wedding photo grimaces, and their fangs gleamed.

Nathan stared at the teeth. He had expected something more dramatic. He didn't say anything for the longest time, and Mikhail and Bianca's eyes darted uncertainly back and forth. As the silence lengthened, their upper lips began to tremble from the strain and a tear squeezed out of the corner of one of Mikhail's eyes.

"So what?" Nathan asked finally. "Those teeth you can probably pick up for ten bucks at a costume shop. I've got a pair at home that look every bit as good as that." It was true. Nathan's teeth had been provided by the cousin of a friend of his brother, who worked in the movie make-up and special effects business. Nathan had worn them to a Hallowe'en party and knew they looked every bit as real, if not more so, that what he was looking at now.

Bianca and Mikhail lowered their lips back over their fangs and Mikhail rubbed his jaw. "You want more proof?" Bianca couldn't entirely hide her displeasure at Nathan's disbelief. It showed in her eyes, but not in her voice. "Very well. Then we need you to do one small thing for us. With your hands."

Involuntarily, Nathan's fingers curled up as he imagined her sucking beads of crimson from their trembling tips. He started to shake, but neither Mikhail nor Bianca moved towards him. Instead she kept talking in her soft, hypnotic way. "Just take your hands," she said, "and place the index finger of one hand over the index finger of the other, at right angles, to make the shape of the...you know...the..." She waved a hand in the air to fill in the word.

"Shape of the cross, you mean," Nathan said. He had never in his life hit a woman, unless you counted Melissa Levinson when he was seven, but simply saying that word made him understand the feeling. Bianca's head snapped back and she grunted as if he had driven a vicious blow to her abdomen.

"Ahh!" Nathan cried. He felt like a heel. "I'm so sorry. I didn't think..."

"It's all right," Bianca said weakly. "Please, when I say ready, make the sign."

She reached over and took Mikhail's hand. They looked at one another again, this time with more sadness than Nathan thought he had ever seen, and then Bianca turned to him and nodded. "Ready." Nathan lifted his hands, index fingers extended, and he made the sign of the cross in the air in front of him.

It was as if a bolt of lightning had blasted from his fingers and hammered the two vampires back into the sofa cushions. They arched their backs and howled, trying desperately to avert eyes that were held riveted to Nathan's fingers. Their faces flushed red and the veins in their necks stood out, pulsing as if they would burst. Nathan stared in awe at the two writhing, groaning wild-eyed figures who squirmed and convulsed before him. He was so mesmerized by what was happening that he forgot for a moment that he was causing it. Then his gaze fell for an instant to his hands and with a cry he yanked his fingers apart as if they were burned. Mikhail and Bianca slumped onto the sofa, leaning panting against one another, tears rolling down their faces as the brilliant red faded, gradually returning them to their usual pallor.

"Wow," Nathan said. "That was something." The question remained, what? It was an impressive display, true. But it could have been acting. It could have been autosuggestion. If these people believed so deeply that they were vampires, they could have this kind of reaction automatically. He figured they probably had the idea so firmly fixed in their minds that if they went outside during the daytime, they'd break out in hives in about five seconds. But there was no way they'd crumble to dust.

As if he read Nathan's thoughts, Mikhail rose and walked toward him. Normally, Mikhail stood very tall and erect. But now he stooped and lumbered forward unsteadily and when he held out his hand it shook as if he were a thousand years old. "I sense you still don't believe. Take my hand."

Nathan reached out unsurely and took hold. If Mikhail was acting, he was awfully good. His grip was still strong and he half pulled Nathan to his feet, then he put his hand around Nathan's shoulder and walked him to a large cloth covered object hanging on the wall. Nathan had figured it was a painting they wanted protected from the sunlight, but Mikhail pulled a cord at the side and the cloth fell away, revealing a large gilt framed mirror.

Nathan stared into it. He felt Mikhail's hand clamped on his shoulder. He felt Mikhail's cool and trembling body next to his own. He heard Mikhail's rasping breath at his ear. But when he looked in the mirror he was quite alone.

Nathan glanced sideways. Mikhail. He looked in the mirror. No Mikhail. He shut his eyes and opened them again. Still no Mikhail in the mirror. "Oh my God," he said. And that's when he broke for the door.

Somehow, Mikhail got there first and Nathan hit him on the dead run. It was like running into a moose. Nathan wound up sitting on the floor, shaking his head in an effort to clear it, and looking up at the imposing vampire who reached a hand down to him. "We will not hurt you," Mikhail said. And he bent down and jerked Nathan to his feet. "We have a deal for you. A proposition."

"What kind of proposition?"

"We want you to supply us with blood," Bianca said in a voice that made Nathan's testicles contract.

Involuntarily, Nathan's hand flew to his neck. Bianca and Mikhail both laughed. "Not from your body, you foolish man," she said. "From where you work. Instead of throwing all that rejected blood away, bring some of it home to us."

"What?" Nathan asked in disgust. "You can't drink that blood."

"Why ever not?" Bianca asked, looking at him in puzzlement.

"Because it's bad. Diseased. It'll make you sick. It'll kill you."

Bianca laughed. "But, Nathan, we're already dead. More or less. What would hurt you can sustain us."

Nathan shook his head. "I don't like it."

"You'll get used to the idea."

"Well," he sighed, "I used to deliver pizzas. I guess it's not really that much different. But why are you doing this?"

"The old way is no good anymore," Bianca said with a wistful smile. "It lacks dignity. And besides, nowadays people aren't as superstitious as they were in the old days. And they all know what they're doing. With the books, and the movies, and on television even, everyone knows about vampires. Do you think if people started showing up with holes in their necks and bloodless veins they wouldn't come after us right away? We'd die horrible, helpless deaths."

"Writhing around with big sticks through our chests," Mikhail added, leaning forward in his seat and jabbing his finger at Nathan's chest for emphasis. "Pinned like butterflies to a cork board. Spewing blood, our eyes bursting." He sat back again, content to let Nathan dwell on the images.

"And don't believe what they say about vampires, either. We don't hate our half-lives, really. We don't have to worry about getting older, about sagging or wrinkles. I haven't coloured my hair in over two hundred and sixty years. And we never have to use aerobics or stair climbers to stay trim. True, we don't tan, but that's no longer good for you anyway. And the diet really isn't bad."

"Oh," Mikhail said, "the diet is wonderful. The variables of blood varietal, vintage and geographic region make for an astounding array of taste sensations. And every so often you hit upon a truly rare specimen and it's an experience any gourmet would sell his soul to sample."

Nathan struggled to control his nausea, the bile pressing frantically against the back of his clenched teeth.

"We just believe in changing with the times," Mikhail said.

"Even vampires have to evolve," added Bianca. "Will you help us?" She looked longingly at him. "If not..." She reached out and ran a cold, soft hand along the side of his neck.

Nathan started supplying blood to the vampires next door the following Monday. Smuggling the tainted samples out was easier than he expected, although with his liquid cargo hidden under his trench coat he felt like it was Prohibition and he was on his way home from the speakeasy.

And, as Bianca had predicted, he did get used to it. That was, in part, because he realized he had no choice. If he didn't supply them with blood, they'd take it. From him. Also, they were being very civilized about the whole thing. Preferring a life of middle class domesticity to one of terrorizing the city and condemning others to their fate.

For well over a year, everything went without a hitch. Nathan delivered every day. The vampires even created a card system. They'd leave one under his door every night, shortly before dawn. It would indicate the order for the day and Nathan would fill it as best he could, noting which particular requests he'd been unable to meet and making it up the following day. He wondered what Mr. O'Sullivan, the milkman he remembered from his youth, clanking from house to house in his white trousers and black bow tie, would think of Nathan and the hideous red pop he delivered now. Lord, how times have changed, Nathan thought to himself as he passed another day's supply into Mikhail and Bianca's eager hands.

Delivering blood got to be as routine as shaving or having lunch. And, after the first half dozen, the parties got to be that way too. But as Nathan's fear diminished, his curiosity increased. And so it was that when the vampires next door announced their latest gathering, Nathan decided he simply had to go, invitation or not.

He knew it would work. For over a year he'd studied two vampires up close. He knew how they talked and acted. He had teeth every bit as good looking as theirs. He knew Mikhail and Bianca would not be happy to see him, but he also knew they wouldn't expose him as an imposter to their friends and risk losing their safe source of supply. He knew the power he had in his fingers, how that simple sign of the cross could immobilize any vampire long enough to let him get away should things go wrong. And he also knew he wouldn't stay long in any event. Pop in, check it out, then head home. A daring commando strike on the vampire bash.

He prepared his apartment as usual with crosses and garlic, for protection when he returned home. He left the door unlocked for quick entry. Then he got himself ready. He wore black Levi's, black western boots, and a grey T-shirt beneath a dusty rose sport shirt. Then, of course, the teeth. He combed his hair and checked the fangs in the mirror, gave himself the thumbs up, and went out into the hallway.

He was about to knock on the vampires' door when a sudden thought occurred to him. Suppose no one arrived this way. Suppose they just materialized from under the door in a puff of smoke, or fluttered through the bedroom window on bat wings. Oh well, he reasoned, those options weren't open to him. So he raised his hand and knocked, hoping no one inside would notice that he hadn't buzzed up from the lobby.

The door was opened almost immediately by a young woman with short orange hair and large gold earrings. "Hi," she said, her kewpie doll eyes studying him and her lips forming a tentative smile. "I only just got here," she said. "It looks like quite a party. I've never been to one of these before."

"Neither have I. Can I come in?"

"Oh, sorry." She stepped back and Nathan entered, jumping in his skin at the sound of the door closing behind him.

"My name's Lucy." Nathan turned to see the orange-haired girl holding out a hand to him. He didn't want to touch her, knowing his hands would be too warm, but he wasn't sure how to avoid it without being rude. Finally he reached out quickly and gave her hand a light swift shake. Her hand felt clammy but she didn't react to the warmth he had feared would give him away.

"Do you know Bianca and Mikhail well?"

Nathan almost blurted out that he'd supplied the blood for the party, but caught himself in time. "Not really. But I better find them and say hello. Excuse me."

He made his way into the apartment. It was full of vampires. For an instant, Nathan had a dreadful thought that they would know automatically that he was not one of them. In the way he'd heard that gays could tell about each other. But there were only the usual casual glances one partygoer gives to another, unfamiliar face. There were vampires on the sofa, leaning against the walls, sitting on the seats and arms of the chairs. It seemed like any normal gathering although everyone was drinking something that looked vaguely like cranberry cocktail and there were

141

no chips and dip in sight.

Nathan headed for the kitchen. As with most of the parties he'd ever been to that was the liveliest room. It was solid vampires, many of them making their way to the two Coleman coolers filled with plasma bags, others pushing their way back through the crowd, drinks held aloft, calling, "Excuse me. Pardon me, please." That was where Nathan abruptly came face to face with Bianca.

At first it was as if she didn't know who he was. He was undoubtedly the last person she ever anticipated seeing at her party so placing him took a while. Then her face drained a shade paler. "What are you doing here?" she hissed.

Nathan smiled, proudly displaying his fangs. "Just checking it out. It's actually pretty dull, just a bunch of half-dead people sitting around talking."

"Many of them haven't seen each other in a hundred years and more. They're catching up. But if you don't leave, this might get more exciting than you'd like."

"I'll be fine," he said, smiling and holding up his two index fingers like six guns.

Bianca shook her head and said simply, "I can't protect you here. No one can. Please, leave now. Before it's too late."

Nathan felt a hand on the small of his back and the chill of it shot through his shirts. "Oooh," a voice murmured, "who's this, Bianca? He's dishy."

Nathan looked around and saw a vampire of about his own age, plunging neckline, short skirt, and dangerously sharp heels. "I'm Ruby," she said. "What's your name?"

"Nathan," he said, reflexively smiling wide enough to show her his fangs.

"You're new," she said.

He nodded. "This is my first party."

"No. New to this, uh, life," she said. "I can always tell."

Suddenly Nathan was overcome by panic. What had he hoped to accomplish? How close was he to being caught? Did Ruby know? Even Bianca couldn't protect him. He turned to her, trying to sound calm. "It was a lovely party. Thanks, but I have to go." Bianca looked at him sadly. "Excuse me."

His impulse was just to shove his way through the crowd, bulldoze to the door. But he knew he'd never make it. He swallowed hard and eased past the revelers as inconspicuously as possible. God, if only he could turn himself into a wisp of smoke and vanish that way. He felt beads of sweat stand out on his forehead and he realized it had never occurred to him before, do vampires sweat? Thinking about it made it worse.

Somehow, Nathan managed to stay calm as he inched forward. The door, though, seemed to have been moved much further away than it was when he came in. It got closer and closer with agonizing slowness as Nathan waded through the blood-drinking throng. He was almost there when he suddenly felt a hand clutch his arm and someone whisper in his ear, with a feral excitement that chilled him, "We've got an imposter."

Nathan froze. If he hadn't been so frightened he would have screamed. He felt tears beginning to build and felt the hand on his arm begin to turn him back until he faced into the apartment. "Come on, Nathan," Ruby said. "Come back. We've got ourselves an imposter."

It took a few seconds for the meaning of the words to sink in. They had an imposter and it wasn't him. There was another one at the party. Nathan almost wept now, but with relief. Unthinkingly, he let Ruby propel him towards the kitchen, and it was only after a few steps that he began to wonder who the other imposter was.

Then, outside the kitchen door, at the centre of a seething knot of vampires, was the orange-haired girl who'd opened the door for him. She was held fast, arms and legs, by at least half a dozen different eager guests. Where their fingers pressed her flesh it showed true vampire white. But her eyes were wide with panic, her mouth open and a terrified keening was all that came out. It made Nathan's knees go weak.

Nathan looked at Ruby whose eyes glittered. "How do you know she's an imposter?" he asked in a whisper.

Ruby didn't take her eyes off the struggling girl. "Someone spilled a glass of blood on her and she used the name of the deity."

It took Nathan some time before he understood this, and he only just stopped himself from repeating the error by muttering aloud, "Oh, she said Jesus Christ." Lucy managed to turn her head in his direction and their eyes met. He tried to give her a look of sympathy but her keening rose in intensity and Nathan understood right away. She recognized him as like her. Perhaps she thought he could help her. Perhaps she thought she could expose him in return for her freedom. He had no idea which.

"How did she get in here?" he asked.

"Doesn't matter. But she's here. And she's ours now. It's always so much better when this happens. And I think she likes you." Then Ruby was moving forward, dragging Nathan with her. "Look out," she said. "Let me through." She drew Nathan up to within three feet of the captive. He could smell her fear.

Then Ruby was talking again, this time to the hungering crowd. "This is Nathan. It's his first party. And he's new. He gets the first bite."

This sent Lucy into a new frenzy of anguished struggle. More hands reached in to hold her fast, two of them gripping her head and wrenching it to the side, exposing the vein on her neck. Her face was flushed red with her terror and her struggling.

Nathan was frozen. Oh God, why didn't he stay home? He extended the index fingers of his hands and looked down at them but knew they were as useless as a water pistol against the horde. They'd simply bring him down from the rear. The door was unreachable, the crowd pressed in around him, and from somewhere a chant went up that built and built as Lucy struggled in vain. "Bite! Bite! Bite! Bite!"

Ruby leaned forward and whispered in Nathan's ear. "Go ahead, Nathan. Bite."

Nathan took one last look around for an avenue of escape but there was none. Then he looked into Lucy's stricken eyes, tried to tell her with his gaze how sorry he was. He stared at the fat vein bulging in the side of her neck. He listened to the ravenous chanting. Bite! Bite! Bite! He said a short and silent prayer. Then Nathan shut his eyes and opened his mouth very wide.

Bombed

Nobody objected at first when Gregoire said they were going to blow up Hannigan.

Nobody objected at all when Gregoire said he would make the bomb and plant it. After all, Gregoire had made and planted bombs all over Montreal and Ottawa back in 1970, during the heady days of the *Front de Libération du Québec.*

True, most of those bombs had never exploded. And two that did had gone off prematurely, one of them blowing the left hand and right arm off the high school student who'd unwittingly been paid five dollars to deliver an unmarked package to the British Consulate.

But that was over twenty years ago when Gregoire had been very young. Since then, he had done time and everyone reasoned that he knew a little more now.

They were sitting in a damp cellar in Toronto sipping cheap French wine from plastic cups. They had come to Toronto because that was where Hannigan lived. It was where Gregoire intended that Hannigan should also die. It was late afternoon and a thin shaft of sunlight slanted in from the one small, high, western facing window. It was the only light. Gregoire insisted on that, and he also insisted on the uncomfortable meeting place. They would all, he said, have to get used to life on the run.

Gregoire knew all about that, too. After the 1970 bombings, he had spent eight months scurrying around Québec, trying to elude the police he thought were pursuing him. They, on the other hand, had assumed he was in Morocco with others of his terrorist cell, and would never have caught him had he not started a violent argument with an Anglo shopkeeper in the Eastern Townships who refused to speak to him in French. Gregoire grew so incensed at *le maudit Anglais* that he punched him in the nose. The local *Sûreté du Québec* arrested him and a routine check showed him to be one of the ten most wanted FLQ terrorists. The officer became an instant hero, as did Gregoire among a different group. And the shopkeeper found his damaged nose and inflated bravery earned him a place at the table, and in the beds, of several available ladies of the area.

But those were the glory days. None of Gregoire's former compatriots would have anything to do with him now. His ideas were too radical. Even at the universities, once hotbeds of unrest, the students were more interested in business careers and job security than in bombing and manifestos and ransom demands.

So they were three. Menard was still there from the old days; his battered beret at a sloppy angle on the right side of his head while a smoking Gauloise balanced it off, dangling perpetually from the left side of his mouth. He was short and plump and his eyes were moist and unhappy.

When Gregoire was in prison, Menard rented a furnished room in Kingston, Ontario, near the federal prison, and waited out the years. He visited Gregoire every week, and on the day Gregoire was released Menard picked him up in a rented car and drove him back to Montreal. All the way, Gregoire could talk only about starting again. The new revolution. How there was no answer but violence and terror. And of Hannigan. Gregoire had read Hannigan's book and his magazine articles, in translations Menard had dutifully composed and provided, and now he was obsessed with the Anglo-Québec ex-patriot. Gregoire had read everything about Hannigan's life. And now he endlessly plotted Hannigan's death.

Dumoulin, an Anglo from Manitoba who did not speak French despite his name, was involved by a stroke of chance. One day he was sitting at a café table next to the one Gregoire and Menard were using.

Their conversation was heated and in French, so Dumoulin could not follow it, but he heard the word *plastique* mentioned several times and that was enough.

At first, when Dumoulin spoke to them softly in English, they ignored him. But when he persisted and told them if they wanted *plastique* he could help, they began to listen. Menard translated for Gregoire who refused to speak, or hear, any English at all.

Dumoulin had been dishonourably discharged from the Canadian armed forces the year before. He had taken with him a lingering hatred for the Canadian government and two pounds of plastic explosive, smuggled out in marble sized balls over a period of ten months. He had simply been waiting for an opportunity to use it in a meaningful way.

He kept one of the small lumps of explosive in his pocket at all times, just in case. To show he was serious, Dumoulin took the explosive out and dropped it on the table between the Québecois conspirators. Menard drew back in shock, hands raised as if to ward off the blast. Even Gregoire was startled. Most of his early bombs had been of dynamite, and he had once blown up a telephone booth with nitroglycerine. He had never even seen *plastique* before, but he had learned all about its properties while in prison. He understood the theory.

Dumoulin laughed as he picked up the formless blob. "Cool it, boys," he said. "This stuff's stable as dirt. You could play handball with it and nothing'd happen. But detonate it" - he smiled and made a soft 'kaboom' with his lips - "and it's good night, nurse."

Gregoire wasn't sure what nurses had to do with anything. After he was through, even doctors wouldn't help, but he let it go. He knew as well as anyone that all Anglos were crazy.

Arrangements were made and Dumoulin took Gregoire and Menard and a golf ball of explosive into the Gatineau hills where he used it to splinter a large maple tree, gouge an enormous divot, and send flocks of birds soaring. "You can get more?" Gregoire asked through Menard, ears ringing.

Dumoulin spoke the only French he knew. "*Oui*," he said with a smile. So Dumoulin became a terrorist and Gregoire became armed and dangerous.

"We'll put the bomb in his car," Gregoire said with a smile. He had put bombs in mail boxes and checked them at bus terminals and placed them outside private homes alongside the morning milk delivery. But he had never put a bomb in a car, and the prospect excited him.

"Timer?" Dumoulin asked.

Gregoire shook his head. "Too risky." He was more cautious now than when he was young. "He might not be in the car when it goes off. I'm going to hook it up to his cell phone. Then we watch and wait and when he takes the car out, we make a business call."

When Dumoulin left to retrieve his cache of *plastique*, Menard stayed behind. There was, after all, still the heel of the bottle. He poured the last of it into his glass too aggressively, and some splashed onto his hand. He licked it off, then expressed his concern to Gregoire, "Do you think this is a good idea?"

"*Quoi?*"

"Blowing up this 'annigan? He's very well known."

"That's exactly the idea," Gregoire slammed his fist on the rickety card table and Menard had to dive forward to keep his wine glass from toppling.

"But won't it bring the authorities after us too seriously? Perhaps we should start small. With a security guard or the nanny of a government official."

"*Tabernac!*"

"A politician, then?" Menard offered meekly.

"We've killed politicians before and what did it change? *Rien*. Nobody cares about them. But 'annigan, the man so many have adopted as the voice of *les maudits Anglais*, his death will cause a stir. His death will let them know that we are to be reckoned with. That separation will not be denied." He fixed Menard with a reptilian glare. "Besides, Menard, who else, other than 'annigan has denounced us in a book on the *New York Times* bestseller list and in American magazines making all Québecois out as buffoons, villains and cowards?"

"*Personne,*" Menard said sadly.

"Who else has attacked us so vehemently, like a coward, from the protective bosom of Toronto?"

"Personne."

"So, who would be a better first strike for us? Whose death would send up a larger cheer all across *la belle province?"*

"Personne."

"Ask me no more stupid questions. It is 'annigan. And it is soon. Is there any more wine?"

∽

Hannigan walked to meet his publisher. It wasn't far, about a mile and a half, and it was one of those perfect autumn days Toronto enjoys. The air was clean and crisp, the sky blue and clear, the leaves a wonderful collage of red and yellow and orange. After the meeting, he'd walk back to get his car and drive to Susan's apartment on the other side of town.

Days like this, Hannigan didn't miss Montreal. The city had changed so much. It was no longer the Montreal in which he grew up. Despite the terrorism of 1970, his disillusionment really began in 1976 with the election of the *Partis Québecois* government and their mandate of separation from the rest of Canada. That disillusionment flourished through the next few years. The Anglophone exodus, mostly to Toronto. The departure of businesses. The draconian laws forbidding any English language signs on store fronts or streets.

He left Montreal initially because he wanted to write about it from a distance; to sense for himself what people outside the province felt about what was going on there. Now he didn't think he could ever return there to live. He kept his summer place in the Eastern Townships, and sometimes he missed the sensual excitement of Montreal at night, but it had changed too much to be his home anymore.

Besides, Susan was here. He whistled aloud and shuffled his feet through the fallen leaves as he walked.

∽

Getting into Hannigan's car was a piece of cake. Gregoire had learned about more than just bombs during his time inside.

Gregoire sat on a bench across the road from Hannigan's condominium, the material for the bomb in a brown paper lunch bag at his side. He sat there patiently for slightly over two hours and, finally, he saw the front door of the building open and Hannigan emerge and stroll briskly along the street without so much as a glance in Gregoire's direction. Gregoire sat ten minutes longer before standing, picking up his lunch bag, and walking casually across the road. He walked along the driveway towards the entrance to the underground garage and after two minutes he heard the automatic door begin to rumble open. Ducking behind a garbage dumpster, Gregoire watched a blue mini-van emerge and, as soon as it had passed him, he broke from cover and sprinted towards the closing door. He raced down the steep ramp and hurled himself under the door moments before it shut.

Rising, he dusted himself off and began looking for Hannigan's license number. It wasn't hard to find. The garage was almost empty. After a quick check to make sure he was unobserved, Gregoire was inside the car in a matter of seconds. He crouched below the dashboard and went to work. The *plastique* he packed under the driver's seat, pushing it securely into the springs. Dumoulin had cautioned him that he had enough of the stuff to demolish a three-storey building, but Gregoire didn't want to take any chances.

"That's a hell of a whoopee cushion," Dumoulin had said. Menard tried to translate, but Gregoire still wasn't sure what *le maudit Anglais* was talking about.

The rest of the installation was simple enough. Gregoire's homemade detonator and two blasting caps were packed into the *plastique* and attached to two fine black wires that led under the passenger seat, then out to the phone where it was positioned over top of the drive shaft. Gregoire tucked the wire as discreetly as possible into the seams in the carpeting, then hooked it up so that the electronic impulse of the phone starting to ring would send a signal snaking down the wire to the detonator, and Hannigan would be annihilated even before he had time to wonder who was calling.

With the bomb in place, Gregoire now had to find the phone number. It wasn't hard. Hannigan, like so many fools, had it written in a small telephone directory in the glove compartment. Gregoire copied it down on a slip of paper, checked it, then checked it again. Satisfied, he eased himself out of the car and locked the door. He arched his back once to stretch out the kinks, walked briskly through the garage, jumped on the cable to open the automatic door, and sauntered out into the sunlight, throwing the empty lunch bag into the garbage dumpster as he passed.

"Why don't we just go back to Montreal, now?" Menard asked. "After all, the bomb is planted. Sooner or later someone will call him and blow him to hell."

Gregoire shook his head. "No," he said. "Someone will not call. I will call. And I'll be in town here when I do it." It was a matter of pride with Gregoire. He had declared war, and he wanted to be the one to push the buttons. And he wanted to hear the immediate reactions of the media first-hand.

⌇

"There was another death threat," Bulivant said, tossing a sheet of paper onto his desk in front of Hannigan.

Hannigan looked at it casually. The content was the same as many of the others, barely comprehensible, but this time it had been done on a personal computer, enlivened with a variety of type faces, to give it more instant visual impact. "It's the prettiest so far," Hannigan said with a smile.

"You can laugh. The police don't think it's funny."

"They've seen this?"

Bulivant nodded. "They have the original. This is a copy."

"We've never got one done on a Mac before, have we?"

"No." Bulivant shook his head. "Look, I'm starting to get nervous. I got into publishing because I thought it would be quiet and safe. Now death threats are arriving at the office every other day, some of them aimed at me. God knows how long before they start sending bombs in padded envelopes marked "Manuscript". I don't know why you find this so amusing, and why you're egging them on."

"I'm not egging them on. But every time something like this arrives it boosts sales. What's the next printing?"

"We just increased it to 75,000."

"That makes four printings and 250,000 books in just over six months. At that rate, I say, keep those cards and letters comin' in, folks. Besides, these guys won't do a damn thing. Trust me. Assassination is like sex. You don't talk about it, you do it. The guys to worry about are the ones you never hear from."

Bulivant shook his head and sighed. "All I need now is to get Salman Rushdie under contract."

"I think the Ayatollah beat you to it," Hannigan said. "Now let's talk about that last royalties statement."

∽

Gregoire never let his small cadre communicate with the media in any way. He certainly wouldn't have permitted direct contact with Hannigan. Let the fools who wrote to Hannigan draw the attention before the fact. After he was dead, then Gregoire would let them know who was really prepared to take action. Who was really to be listened to. Who was really to be feared. So, no. No threats in the mail. No contact with the quarry. The only time they'd even come close to that would be that one fatal phone call.

Gregoire placed that call for the first time later that afternoon. From their vantage point outside Hannigan's apartment, Gregoire and Menard watched him drive away and then they walked as casually as the circumstances allowed to a nearby public telephone. Gregoire fished in his pockets for a quarter but found none. "Have you a quarter?" he asked Menard.

Menard frowned and fumbled through his pockets, eventually digging out a coin. Gregoire slipped it into the phone and carefully dialled the number he'd copied down on his sheet of paper. After dialling he waited in eager expectation for the phone to start to ring.

He wondered what would happen when the explosion came. Would he be cut off in mid-ring? Would he feel some trembling vibration down the line? Or, and this would be the best of all, would a clinical computer-generated voice come on the line and announce, "We're sorry, the number you have dialled is no longer in service."

Gregoire was so engrossed in these thoughts that he didn't immediately notice that the first ring was not cut off. Nor was the second. Nor the third. And the voice that answered the phone in the middle of the fourth ring wasn't generated by computer, but by a cheerful woman who said, "Hello?"

Gregoire was stunned. He couldn't figure out what was happening. He couldn't think of anything to say.

"Hello?" the voice said again. "Is anyone there?"

Gregoire held the phone as far away from his face as the phone booth would allow and stared at it in a mixture of confusion and irritation. From a distance, he heard the woman's voice repeat, "Hello? Hello?" Then she hung up and the phone in Gregoire's hand began to buzz. After a few more seconds, he slammed it down and left the phone booth.

"What happened?" Menard asked.

Gregoire stared at Menard as if he didn't know who he was. Then he said, *"Je ne sais pas."*

"There was something wrong with the bomb?"

"No, *trou d'cul*, there's nothing wrong with the bomb. There's something wrong with that phone. It misdialled on me. Or there's something wrong with the phone company. They misdirected my call. But the bomb is perfect."

"Perhaps you copied the number down wrong," Menard suggested gently.

"Tabernac!" Gregoire exploded, and Menard spat the butt of his Gauloise to the sidewalk and fumbled for a fresh one. "We will try again from another phone."

Two blocks along the street Gregoire and Menard found another phone booth. Gregoire took the slip of paper with Hannigan's phone number on it from his pocket and stared hard at it, frowning. Menard patted his pockets again in search of another quarter but found nothing.

"Rien," he said to Gregoire.

"Well let's go and get one," he said, walking briskly away. Menard stuffed his hands into his pockets and shuffled along behind. They stopped in a doughnut shop and Menard bought them each a day-old cruller. He paid with a five-dollar bill, giving Gregoire a quarter from the change, and Gregoire went to the phone on the wall beside the exit.

Gregoire studied the number one last time before dialling. He punched the digits slowly and carefully.

This time he didn't think about what might happen on the other end of the line. He restrained himself from visions of twisted metal and severed limbs and focused instead on what he could hear. The musical tone of the number dialling, the crackling pause while he waited for the connection, and then the ringing. Once. Twice. Three times. And the same woman's voice abruptly on the end of the line, "Hello?"

Gregoire was stunned, but this time he knew he had to say something, but what? He hadn't spoken English in such a long time. Suddenly, unable to stop himself, he blurted out, "Are the pants ready?"

This time the silence was on the other end of the line. Then the woman's voice came back, bemused, "Pants? I'm afraid you have the wrong number."

"Moi aussi," Gregoire said. *"Excuse-moi."* And he slammed down the phone, cursing. He knew he hadn't misdialled. This time he knew the phone company had made a mistake. Maybe he should blow them up next. He left the doughnut shop hurriedly and Menard darted after him, brushing crumbs from his shirt.

"No luck?" Menard asked.

"It's not a question of luck," Gregoire snapped. "Something is not right."

"Are you going to try again?" Menard asked sadly.

"Later. Now I need a glass of wine and time to think."

Menard's expression brightened noticeably.

∽

The third time the phone rang in Susan Bellamy's apartment, she picked it up hesitantly. The last two calls had been odd and curiously unsettling. True, there'd been no heavy breathing or guttural obscenities, unless you considered a bizarre request about pants obscene. But there was still something not quite right. Susan picked up the receiver on the third ring. "Hello?" she said after a moment's pause.

Then she did hear breathing, what sounded like a sigh of disappointment, and the same thick French accent from before asked, "Is Guillaume there?"

"No," she said. "There's no one here by that name."

The voice sighed again and rattled off a telephone number, interspersing English and French digits, asking if that was the number he had called. Susan wasn't exactly sure what number he'd quoted, but she recognized enough to know it wasn't hers. "No," she said. "I'm afraid you've got the wrong number." Then she hung up, very puzzled indeed.

∽

"I've had a couple of phone calls," Susan said after she'd shut the door behind Hannigan and kissed him for a very long time.

"What do you mean?"

"Three, actually. It was very peculiar."

"What was it, a heavy breather?"

"No, it was some guy with a French accent. The third time he called he asked for Guillaume. That's French for William."

"I thought it was French for bean."

"That's *légume*," she said.

"Ah, so he asked for Guillaume, did he?"

"Yes, but then he gave me the number he'd dialled, to check, you know? And usually when people do that, they're off by one digit or they've transposed a couple of numbers, or something. But the number he gave me wasn't even close. It didn't make sense at first, but the number seemed familiar. After I hung up, I realized it was your cell phone number."

She frowned. "You might have told me you were forwarding your calls here. I could have taken a message or helped the guy out."

"It's just as well you didn't," Hannigan said. "There was another death threat."

"Oh, Bill," she gave him a worried look.

"Don't worry. It's no big deal. Just another crank who wants to shoot off his mouth. The ones who are serious about it don't want to talk about it."

"But your cell phone number isn't listed. How did they get it?"

Hannigan shrugged. "Bribe somebody. Blackmail somebody. Sleep with somebody. Find some ten-year-old whiz kid computer hacker to break into the data base. There are more ways than you could imagine to find out just about anything you want to know."

"So what are you going to do about it?"

"Nothing. Go out for dinner. Have a nice bottle of wine."

"I don't know how you can be so casual about this." She held out her hand. "Look, I'm shaking."

"Glass of wine'll fix you right up. Calm you right down."

"French?"

"Naw. A nice Ontario riesling."

∽

Gregoire's newest weapon was a cellular phone of his own. It hadn't been his idea. Dumoulin had simply shown up with it soon after the first failed attempt on Hannigan's life. It was very small, folding neatly in half. Gregoire took it from Dumoulin and slipped it into his pocket.

"Pour vous," Dumoulin said in his ever expanding French. "I decided to do some research," he continued in English which Menard translated slowly, "to find out what the hell was going on. He's probably having his calls forwarded."

Gregoire and Menard looked blank.

"It's technology, man," Dumoulin continued. "Hannigan has something programmed into the phone so that when you call his number, the call is intercepted and it rings somewhere else. It doesn't ring in the car. So the bomb won't go off."

Gregoire and Menard still said nothing. "That's why I got the phone," Dumoulin told them. He went on to explain that now someone could watch Hannigan and as soon as he was in the car, the watcher could call Gregoire and Gregoire could detonate the bomb wherever he was. Eventually, Hannigan would switch the call forwarding off and they'd have him.

Gregoire took the small phone out and unfolded it, turning it over lovingly in his hands. He appreciated the potential, and also the fact that it was registered in Dumoulin's name and he would get the bills. Here was power. Small and lethal. The ability to communicate instantly with anyone from anywhere. He decided to put it to the test. He would call his mother in Trois Rivières. He hoped he could remember the number.

⁓

Susan was in the kitchen when Hannigan woke up. After dinner they'd walked back to her place and Hannigan hadn't gone home. He brushed past her and poured a cup of coffee.

"Do you need your car this morning?" Susan asked.

"No. Why?"

"I have a few errands to run. Mind if I borrow it?"

"Sure. I've got this article that's due in two days and I haven't started writing yet. If I'm here and you're out I can get some work done."

"Not another scathing blast at separatist policies, I hope."

"You know me better than that," he said with a smile.

She took his keys and left.

She liked Hannigan's car. It handled smoothly and offered steady, even acceleration. It had FM and a CD player, while her clunker was restricted to noisy AM stations. She eased back in the plush seat, adjusted the rearview mirror, altered the tilt of the steering wheel, and started the engine smoothly and easily. Then she switched the radio from jazz to classical. Susan enjoyed the phone, too. She liked the convenience of it and the fact that if she ever broke down on the highway she could get help quickly. She also liked the fact that Hannigan had it set up so that you didn't have to pick the phone up to talk. It always horrified her to see people barrelling along at great speeds, one hand on the wheel and the other clamping a phone to the side of their head. Before she backed out of the parking spot at the side of her building, she switched on Hannigan's phone and dialled the number of her apartment.

"Yeah?" Hannigan said, with the gruff abruptness he always had when he was disturbed at work.

"It's only me, Tolstoy," she said. "I just wondered if you wanted me to pick anything up for you?"

"Don't think so, thanks. Oh, and listen, turn off the call for-warding for me, will you? I don't want the phone ringing here while I'm trying to work. Calls that I know are for you I can ignore. But if I think they're for me, I'll have to answer and I'll never get this thing done."

"Should I take messages for you?" she asked.

"You can. Or you can just let it ring. Or you can just switch the phone off entirely. Whatever. Now let me get back to work."

"I'll leave it on," she said. "You may change you mind. Or I may just call up all my relatives in Australia."

∽

It was warm in the mid-morning sunshine and Menard had drunk most of a litre of red wine at breakfast. He sat half dozing on the bench in the park across the street from Susan Bellamy's apartment building. It wasn't a building really. Not tall and gleaming like Hannigan's. It was a house, renovated into three flats. Menard had no idea who lived there, but Dumoulin had followed Hannigan the night before and this was where he ended up. He was still in there, according to Dumoulin, who had been wide awake despite being on watch most of the night.

Keeping watch was easy here because there was no underground parking. Hannigan's car stood in plain sight, gleaming in the bright sun on the paved parking pad at the side of the house. Menard had watched the car steadily for hours and his eyes were beginning to ache. He rubbed them and yawned. There had been no sign of Hannigan. No activity of any kind. And he was feeling so contented with the wine and the gentle breeze from the lake and the spikes of sunshine through the leaves. He needed to rest his eyes. He'd shut them for just a second.

The dog woke Menard. It bounced up and down at his feet, yapping angrily. Menard started and opened his eyes wide, looking around wildly, imagining himself surrounded by police with gas masks, riot guns and German shepherds. But all Menard saw was one small mottled mongrel and he sent it yelping away with a sharp kick. Then he took a deep breath to stop his heart pounding, rubbed the sleep from his eyes, and resumed his watch. He knew right away that something was different. It just took him a few minutes to figure out exactly what. When he did, it drove the air from his lungs in a gasp. Hannigan's car was gone.

Frantically, he looked up the street, then down, praying he would see it just rounding the corner or waiting at a stop sign. But there were no cars in sight at all.

How long had the vehicle been gone, he wondered desperately? How long had he slept? Had it been a minute or a hour? He looked up to the sun as if he could read the time, but he had no idea which way was east and even if he did, he realized it would have been useless. He knew all he needed to know. The car was gone. The hare was out. And the hounds had been caught napping.

Gregoire had trained Menard long ago not to run. People notice a running man, Gregoire said. Walk quickly and with purpose. For twenty years, that's what Menard had done. But now panic overtook everything he'd learned and, clamping a hand on top of his beret, he ran.

Menard leaned panting against the phone booth as he fished for a quarter and dropped it in the slot. He punched the numbers too quickly in his excitement, hanging up, redialling the number of Gregoire's portable phone. *"Vite, vite,"* Menard muttered to himself as he waited for the connection. He bounced up and down in agitation. He didn't realize at first that the line was busy. Finally the buzzing made itself understood and

Menard slammed down the phone.

"*Mon hosti de putaine,*" he muttered and lit another Gauloise with anxious fingers.

∽

By eleven o'clock, Hannigan was fed up. The article wasn't going well. He'd written a dozen different openings, none of which was right. He was having trouble focusing and decided he needed a break. He knew just what to do. The kind of shopping excursion Susan was on today followed a predictable pattern. He was willing to bet that he knew exactly where she was at that very minute. He'd surprise her, perhaps find the car unoccupied and wait for her in the passenger seat. They'd have lunch together and he'd finish the article in the afternoon.

Shutting off the portable computer, Hannigan stood and stretched, grabbed his keys and his wallet, and went outside to hail a cab. As he settled back on the stiff, cracked upholstery, he looked out and saw a short, fat man in a beret stagger up to a phone booth and lean against it heavily. For a brief second, Hannigan wondered what his hurry was. Then he turned his thoughts to Susan and the panting man was forgotten.

∽

Susan drove slowly past the row of parked cars, looking for a space. Usually there were plenty to be had at curbside along this ten-block stretch of shops and restaurants. But today everything was taken. As she searched, Susan realized Hannigan was right and she shouldn't worry about the death threats. But these phone calls were different. They were very direct and very personal and there was something unsettling about them. Whoever had called obviously knew Hannigan's cellular number, but not his unlisted home number. What did they want? Absently, she took her right hand off the wheel, reached out, and tapped her fingers on Hannigan's phone.

༽

Menard tried again. He fumbled the quarter into the slot and hesitated. He could dial Hannigan's number himself. He was sure he remembered it, having watched Gregoire punch out the numbers so many times. Then he could claim that someone else must have called and the resulting explosion, and Hannigan's death, were serendipity. But no. Menard knew himself. He knew that killing someone was not in him. He hadn't the stomach for it. The same failing that had kept him from climbing higher up the ranks of the FLQ. He dialled Gregoire.

༽

Susan drove past the store she wanted, turned at the next corner and began slowly circling back around the long series of blocks.

༽

"Allo," Gregoire's voice crackled over the phone on the second ring. Menard could hear music and conversation in the background. Gregoire was obviously at that little bistro he liked so well.

"He's out," Menard blurted. "He's gone. He's in the car."

"Bon," Gregoire said, and the phone clicked and hummed in Menard's ear. Thank Christ the responsibility was now out of his hands. He walked away from the phone booth and began looking for a place where he could sit quietly and have a glass of wine. Then he remembered it was Toronto and the bars did not begin serving until eleven thirty, and he cursed Hannigan at length.

༽

Hannigan rolled down the back window of the cab and the freshness of the autumn air poured in. He loved the climate in Canada. True, the winters in Toronto weren't as dramatic as in Montreal, but the feeling he got from the changing seasons was exhilarating. Let other Canadians head for Florida or California where the difference between January and July was negligible. This was his country and he loved it.

∽

Susan wasn't having any luck at all. There were still no parking spots on her side of the street on her second pass. Once, she saw one on the other side but it was taken before she could make a U-turn. So she drove along to the next street and continued her slow circling.

∽

Gregoire picked up his change and went outside the bistro. The sun was shining and the cloudless sky was as blue as the *fleur-de-lis* on the flag of Québec. It was a perfect day, and it was about to get better. As he strolled along the sidewalk, past convenience stores and dry cleaners and gift shops, he reached into his pocket and took out the piece of paper on which he'd written Hannigan's number. He knew it by heart, but he wanted to make sure. There had been enough mistakes already. He checked the number, put the paper back in his pocket and, standing on the sidewalk as the traffic hummed in his ears, he began to dial slowly. He muttered *"Maudite pelote,* 'annigan," and laughed, causing a woman to walk by him with an uncomfortable look.

∽

Circling the block a third time, Susan experienced the miracle that sometimes happens to city drivers. Someone was just pulling out of a metered space directly across the street from the store she was heading to. She stopped behind the spot, signalled her intention, and waited while the other driver pulled slowly away.

~

The cab dropped Hannigan off near the shop he knew Susan would be visiting last. He looked up and down the street, on both sides, scanning the people on the street for Susan's familiar face. Not finding it, he turned his attention to the cars parked at the curb and those crawling past looking hopefully for a place of their own. At first he missed it, obscured by a garbage truck. But then a traffic light changed and the truck chugged ahead and Hannigan saw his car across the road and down the block. He stepped onto the street and started towards it quickly.

~

Gregoire knew something hadn't gone right. The pause between dialling and ringing was too long. He hoped that didn't mean that somebody else had already called through and robbed him of the pleasure of killing Hannigan himself. Of course, he'd still take credit since the bomb was his and he'd taken the risk of planting it, but there'd always be an empty place inside him that knew he hadn't seen the job through. Angrily, he terminated the call and redialled, pushing each number slowly and aggressively.

~

Hannigan was almost halfway across the street when the explosion came. His eyes had been darting back and forth from his car to the traffic around him to the sidewalk, to see if Susan was anywhere in sight. He had just fixed his gaze back on the car when it erupted in flame and a shower of debris. There was a noise that battered against his ears like the right hands from two heavyweights and a concussion that hammered on his chest like a gong. The next thing he knew, he was sitting on the road surrounded by honking cars and screaming people. His own car, just moments before parked peacefully at the curb, was now a blackened hulk. Its charred body was blown half onto the sidewalk, while the roof lay on top of the crushed hood of a passing Chevrolet. It smouldered and smoked and occasional tongues of flame licked skyward.

"Oh my God," he screamed aloud. "Susan!"

He stood and found that something was wrong with his right leg, for it nearly collapsed under him. Adjusting for the injury, he limped forward as fast as he could, panic rising with every step.

"Susan," he called out over and over, his voice mingling with the screams and cries of dozens of others in an aria of fear. Then he saw her. She came out of the food store and stood in front of the shattered window. He lurched towards her, still calling her name. She saw him then, too, and dropped her bag of groceries and ran forward. He wrapped his arms around her and squeezed her in relief. He pressed his face into her hair, shut his eyes, and for a brief second wondered what had happened to the man who'd been standing beside the car when it exploded. The man who'd been making a call on his cellular phone.

Last Resort

Barker was late getting away again and he drove all night. He stopped once at the side of the Massachusetts Turnpike and slept in the car for an hour and a half, and then he pressed on. He drove much faster than the 55-mile-an-hour limit, but he didn't figure there'd be many state troopers out looking for speeders at four o'clock in the morning. He made it to Hyannis just as the sun was coming up.

He parked his car at the Kennedy Memorial and sat on one of the curved stone benches watching the day begin. Seagulls swirled above him, landing on the beach and the grass, vainly struggling crabs clenched in their beaks. A middle-aged couple jogged past and waved, and a few minutes later a woman strolled by in the company of a large black Lab. After half an hour, Barker went back to his car. He knew Harris well, so he knew he'd be awake.

Barker drove slowly the last few hundred yards to Oceanview. He passed Veteran's Park to his left and the bird sanctuary to his right and followed the road as it curved to the west. Oceanview was right there. Two four-unit buildings at the water's edge. Their situation was perfect. Ocean to the south, beach to the east, bird sanctuary to the north and, to the west, large private homes. Even on the crowded Cape, Oceanview gave you the impression of solitude.

Barker had been right. Harris was up. He was standing on the low stone wall near the steps that led down to the small private beach, a steaming mug of coffee in his hand. The wind tossed Harris's blond hair around and blew the steam from the mug wildly to the side. He turned when he heard Barker's tires crunch over the gravel. Barker parked next to a German-made car that also had Ontario plates and climbed out.

"You want a coffee?" Harris asked as Barker drew up beside him. "You look like you could use it."

"Thanks. I could also use a couple hours' sleep."

"Pulled an all nighter again, eh?"

Barker shook his head. "One of these days I'll get away in time and make it here at a civilized hour. Like just in time for a cocktail."

"Buddy," Harris said, "you're on vacation. It's always time for a cocktail."

Barker had that first drink of the day in the unit he'd be using for the next week. It was the southernmost second floor unit of the southernmost building. It had an unobstructed view, both south and east, and Barker thought he could happily stay there forever. He sipped the spiked coffee slowly. Harris had laced it with a stiff shot of brandy and Barker could feel the tension from eleven hours of driving easing out of his shoulders. It was good to be back.

"So how's the ad biz?" Harris asked with a chuckle. "Crazy as ever?"

"Oh yeah," Barker said, although he didn't want to talk about work. "What about the resort game?"

"Resort," Harris laughed. "'Bout the same. Half full this week, half empty next."

"You got all eight units open yet?"

Harris shook his head. "Two are still out of commission, but I hope by next season."

"Can you hang on?"

Harris shrugged. "Dunno. It'll be tight. The bank says they won't loan me any more." Then he smiled. "But I'm still in there swinging."

"Many of the regulars here?"

"Some. The Snells. Jessica Smith's here, too."

"With her husband?"

Harris nodded and grinned. "He's up in Boston at the moment, but he'll be back."

"He wouldn't be who you're thinking of asking for money, by any

166

chance?" Jeremy Smith was the manager of a bank in Boston who'd taken an interest in Oceanview. But Harris had always said he didn't feel right about approaching him for a loan.

"I have to do something," Harris said. "It's awful tight."

Barker figured that was an understatement. Harris had bought Oceanview in a weak moment and in a hurry. Burned out by too many years in the ad business, too many impossible deadlines and too many unreasonable clients, he'd jumped in the car one morning and headed across the border, ending up on Cape Cod. He'd never been there before and it was love at first sight. It was still early in June when he arrived, so finding a place to rent for a week wasn't a problem. He found Oceanview early that evening and paid cash in advance for one of the available units. Five days of staring out over the ocean, walking on the beach and sipping cold Stroh's was working hard to undo the knot in his stomach. On the sixth day, he found out the whole place was about to go up for sale. The owner told Harris he'd thought about going condo with it, but decided to unload it instead and just retire. Harris thought about it for a minute, then said simply, "I'll buy it."

They discussed it for a long time, but Harris's mind was made up. And the same tenacity that made him so good at defending his ideas back at the agency made him stick to this idea too. The real estate agent drew up the papers, Harris agreeing to pay the full asking price with no conditions. He arranged for a deposit through a local bank and then headed back to Toronto to sell his house and make all the other arrangements.

The Toronto real estate market collapsed the week Harris put his house up for sale. It stayed on the market for months and when it did sell it was for much less than he'd dreamed possible. Right from the start, Oceanview put Harris in the hole.

But it was what he wanted to do. He told all this to Barker as he was cleaning out his office, disposing of the detritus of fifteen years in advertising. For eight of those years, he and Barker had been partners. At one time, according to one of the industry magazines, they were among the top three creative teams in the city. Now that was over.

Harris drew up a map and promised to hold one of the units for Barker for two weeks in July. He said Barker would love it too, and he was right.

It wasn't until Harris was almost back on the Cape, everything he was taking stuffed into the trunk and tossed carelessly on the back seat, that he realized he'd never even looked at the second building.

The owner had said it was just a slow time of year and it was better to have all the guests in one building. Now Harris, his heart sinking, understood why no one had lived there during his stay. The building he'd stayed in had been recently renovated - badly, he was to discover later - but the other had not. It still boasted lead plumbing ready to burst in several spots and wiring that had been untouched since construction. The seventy-year-old plaster bulged from the walls and the wind roared through cracks and gaps.

Already stretched to the limit, Harris couldn't afford to repair the units right away and he wasn't able to do it himself. He limped along from one payment to the next for five years, slowly putting away enough cash to bring the new building up to standard one unit at a time. Now only two remained to be done, but there was no more money to be borrowed. Harris was more worried than Barker had ever seen him.

"So who's that from the old country?" Barker asked from the window.

"The Ontario plates? Guy named Merrill. He's a contractor, handy-man type. Been here a week already and he's doing some work for me. He's working on Jessica, too. You'll meet later."

Barker nodded and yawned. "I think I'm gonna sack out for an hour or two. Got my key?"

Harris fished it from his pocket, tossed it to Barker and went to the door. When Harris had gone, Barker dropped on the bed, and it was almost cocktail hour by the time he woke up.

∽

Barker stood on the deck of Harris's condo and looked out across the ocean. The wind tugged at his shirt and tried to blow away what was left of his hair, but after the heat and humidity of Toronto it felt refreshing and calming. He sipped his beer and watched the windsurfers zigzag across the snapping whitecaps off the public beach.

"Nice to see you again," a voice said not far from his left ear.

Barker turned to look at Jessica Smith. She was wearing a light summer dress that the wind plucked at and lifted coyly, like an adolescent trying to catch a glimpse. Seeing the flashes of long tanned leg, Barker could understand why. She looked better than he remembered, and he remembered she looked awfully good.

"Too windy," she said. "Let's go in."

Barker hung back for a few seconds, watching the colourful sails scooting back and forth in the distance against the choppy green of the water and the crisp blue of the sky, then he went in too. Most Saturday nights, Harris had as many guests as cared to come into his place for a casual drink. Barker had seen such gatherings with as many as fifteen people and as few as Harris and himself sitting on the deck, watching the ocean and getting quietly crocked. It was a continuation of something Harris used to do in his agency days in Toronto when, every Friday at four, he hosted what he called Happy Hour in his office. Then, though, it was strictly BYOB.

There were six of them this time. Jessica was standing next to Ian and Betty Snell, both doctors from New York who were Oceanview regulars. There was a guy on his own, talking with Harris, who Barker took to be Merrill.

Barker went up to the Snells and they shook hands. Barker enjoyed talking with them, particularly Ian, who was always anxious to discuss advances in medical research and surgical technique with anyone who'd listen.

Ian was about to fill Barker in on a new development in post mortem identification when Jessica came over and placed a hand on Barker's arm. "I was hoping you'd be back," she said.

Barker sipped his drink. "I was hoping the same thing," he said.

"That I'd be back?"

"That I would. How's Jeremy?"

"He's Jeremy. Business could be going better. The economy has taken its toll, but things certainly could be worse." She paused, then added,

"They may get that way soon. Harry asked him for money, you know."
She frequently referred to people in the diminutive, which Barker found
curiously insulting.

"Did Jeremy go for it?"

She shook her head. "He might consider buying the place outright,
as an investment, because he'd be able to put the money into it that it
needs, but the way things are he won't put the bank's money on the line.
Harry's too bad a risk; unless Jer's intention was to give him the money so
he could eventually foreclose and then buy the property back from the
bank for a song. But Jeremy's too ethical for that." She said it as if ethics
were sort of like scabies.

Barker noticed that Merrill was watching Jessica carefully from across
the room. He looked to be about thirty, with dark eyes and well defined
cheekbones. It seemed that a guy just like him showed up at Oceanview
every year. The same time as Jessica. "So who's this guy Merrill?"

"He's from Toronto, too," she said softly. She pronounced every
syllable carefully, unlike a native who'd slur it out as Trawno.

"Some kind of handyman?"

"Mmhmm. Very. He took care of a little plumbing problem for
me last week when Jer was back in Boston on some crisis or other."

"It's nice to have helpful neighbours." Barker finished his drink.
"I've gotta go into town and pick up some groceries. You need anything?
Or does Merrill have it covered?"

"You're wicked," she said.

"That makes two of us."

～

Barker hit the Stop 'n Shop and walked out with four bags of groceries.
Then he went to a nearby liquor store for half a dozen bottles of wine
and four six-packs of Miller. Finally, at a hardware store he picked up a
bunch of things Harris needed. He figured he'd spend the next morning
putting in a couple of dimmer switches and popping a washer into a

leaky faucet and then, if there wasn't too much wind, he'd try his hand at windsurfing.

He dropped by at Harris's and gave him one of the six-packs.

"Nightcap?" Harris asked.

"Sure." Barker took the opened beer and drank it from the bottle. "So what's the story with our Jessica and this guy Merrill?"

"You always cut right to the chase," Harris laughed.

"The question is, though, who's chasing who?"

"She's just playing her little game while Jeremy's in Beantown. He'll be back tomorrow and she'll cool her jets."

"She said you asked him to bail you out and he turned you down cold."

Harris shrugged. "There's still a chance. I think he liked the idea a bit, and I'm going to try him again when he gets back. I don't know what else to do."

"You'd do anything to keep the place."

Harris spread his arms wide. "Look around. I'd kill somebody to keep it."

"Kill somebody?"

Harris thought for a minute, then said, "Well, maybe I'd punch him real hard."

‿

The next day the wind blowing in from Nantucket and Martha's Vineyard was harder than ever and, after taking care of the chores using some tools Harris had borrowed from Merrill, Barker decided windsurfing was out of the question. He was just throwing his beach gear into the car when Jessica walked up to him.

"Where you going?" she asked.

"Thought I'd drive up to Marconi Beach for the day." He slammed the trunk.

"Want company?"

"What about old Jer?"

171

"He won't be back till tonight. Hang on, I'll get my things." She ran inside and reappeared a few minutes later, climbing into the front passenger seat. Barker started the engine.

The wind through the open window played with Jessica's hair and what was left of Barker's. She popped a Chet Baker tape into the cassette player and sang along. "Let's get lost, lost in each other's arms."

"I bet you say that to all the boys," Barker said.

She laughed. "Only to you."

"What about Merrill?"

"Are you still on that kick? There's nothing between me and Merrill, and I've never been unfaithful to Jeremy. Besides, I've only ever thought about that with you."

"Flatterer."

∽

As they climbed down the wooden steps to Marconi Beach the wind fell away, blocked by the high bluffs. On the sand it was very hot. They walked a long way down the beach, away from the families with kids and the young lovers, and Barker spread out a towel.

He'd packed a lunch and they ate it looking out over the water at the horizon. Every so often a sail would appear, slicing through the brilliant, infinite blueness of the sky and then it would disappear again like a mirage. They walked along the beach, the surf rolling in and soaking them to their knees. Once, a wave washed a starfish up on shore in front of them and Jessica picked it up, feeling how soft and pliant it was.

"It's still alive," she said, and she reached out to gently drop it back in the water.

"It'll probably just get washed back again," Barker said. "Then some seagull'll have it for lunch or a kid'll take it home and pin it to a cork board."

"At least this way it'll have one more chance. Who knows how it'll turn out?"

At three o'clock she said, "We better head back. I want to be there when Jer gets home."

As it turned out, she was too late.

～

When Barker pulled into the Oceanview parking lot, they could see Jeremy's car. And as they got out, they could hear Jeremy's voice carried on the wind. It was loud and very angry.

"God damn it, I told you before I left that it was out of the question. Don't you understand that? Out of the question. No can do. Impossible. Now, I'm here to enjoy my vacation and if you don't leave me alone and stop bugging me about this, we're packing up and you're giving me back the rest of our rent money. And I'll litigate you into the ground to get it."

Jessica looked at Barker over the roof of the car. "Whoops," he said.

Jeremy came around from the front of the building, head down and nostrils flaring. He glowered at Jessica. "Where the hell have you been?" Opening his trunk and hauling out an elaborate brown leather suitcase, he went on, "I wasn't here two minutes and he was on me like a bad smell. Jesus." He puffed inside and slammed the door behind him. Jessica followed without a word.

Barker went looking for Harris. He found him standing by the low stone wall, looking out at the ocean.

"What the hell was Smith so steamed up about?" Barker said. "Did you ask him for dough again?"

Harris shrugged.

"You never did know how to pick your spots, pal. It's like trying to sell an ad to a suit who's just got reamed out by the client for something he didn't do. You'd barge right in and try anyway, and you always got shot down."

"Not always."

"Mostly. He probably had a lousy day in Boston. He probably had a lousy drive back. He was probably figuring Jess'd be waiting for him with his slippers and a beer. He was in a lousy mood. And you just dove right in."

"I can't wait anymore. I'm dying on the vine here. I don't see any other way. If he won't help me out I may as well torch the place for the insurance money." Barker shuddered at the image and Harris kicked sand and stones in front of him as he walked back through the parking lot.

As Harris walked away, Merrill drifted out of one of the untenanted units, brushing plaster dust off his trousers in great grey clouds.

"Hiya," he said as he saw Barker walking towards him. He was younger than Barker and he had more hair. It was blond and wavy and had bits of plaster in it. "Boy, Harry's in a bit of a state." Somehow hearing Merrill use Jessica's choice of diminutive irked Barker a lot. "I guess it was having Jessie's old man light into him the way he did."

"You heard that, eh?"

Merrill nodded and chunks of plaster flew out of his hair like shrapnel. "Hard not to. I'm redrywalling the top floor and doing a little work on the plumbing, and with the windows open and the wind blowing in it was like they were standing in the next room." He reached into the open trunk of his car and took out a battered metal tool case and a plastic hardware store bag. "Saw you coming back with Jess. What a doll. Good thing her old man came back when he did, 'cause another day or two and I couldn't've been held responsible for what happened. She's something, wouldn't you say?"

Barker didn't say and Merrill's brilliant smile faded a little. "No offence, of course," he said. "Anyways, Harry's got himself a hell of a place here. Once I get it fixed up for him, that is." He chuckled. "I sure hope he can hang onto it. Well, back to the salt mines." And he hefted the toolbox and the bag and headed back inside.

Barker watched him go, and still didn't say a word.

⌇

The wind died down early in the evening.

Jessica invited everybody to a barbecue to celebrate the fact that Jeremy was back. She corralled Barker into lighting the 'cue, an old charcoal burning relic that took a couple of quarts of lighter fluid and a pack of matches to ignite. Huddled over it in the lee of one of the buildings, Barker longed for a gas model. But finally it caught and he left the coals to grow hot as he pulled up a few deck chairs and brought down a dozen beers.

Jessica came with the steaks and the swordfish. Merrill brought a bottle of California wine with dust on it. Barker figured he coated it with plaster dust just to give it that vintage look. Harris brought foil wrapped potatoes and Ian and Betty Snell brought a pie that each claimed the other had baked. Jeremy brought his bad temper.

There were enough people there, and enough to drink, that everything was relaxed and mellow. The food was good and, Barker admitted reluctantly, so was Merrill's bottle of wine. The sky darkened quickly and Barker marveled again at the number of stars you could see on the Cape at night. Vainly, he hunted out the various constellations but gave up after finding one of the dippers. He wasn't sure if it was the big or little one.

A couple of times, he also noticed Merrill's hand drifting over to Jessica's leg and she pushed it away as casually as she could with a quick glance at her husband. Barker wasn't sure whether Jeremy noticed or not. Once he missed it because Harris was talking to him, using a lot of urgent, clenched fist gestures, and Barker couldn't tell if it was just falling night or if Jeremy's expression had darkened.

Sometime after ten the party broke up. Jessica was the first to leave, asking Jeremy if he'd like to walk with her a little. His reply was curt and clear: he was going to bed. As he stalked away he turned to Merrill and growled, "Stay the hell away from my wife."

Merrill's smile glowed in the darkness. "Screw you," he said.

When Jeremy was gone, Jessica started off alone. Then everyone else gathered up what they'd brought and trundled off into the darkness.

Barker picked up his empties and folded the deck chairs, throwing some water on the coals to make sure they were out.

〜

An hour later, Barker was sitting on the deck with the outside light turned off, his feet resting on the top railing and a steaming mug of tea in his hand. The wind had died down almost entirely now and he could hear the invisible ocean lapping on the shore. He had just about decided that he'd found Orion's belt when he heard the screaming.

It was coming from the building to the west and it was definitely a woman. Then the door to the Smiths' unit flew open and a figure raced out of the doorway, still screaming. Barker could tell from the voice now, and from the wild mane of hair flowing in the dim light that spilled out of the still open doorway, that it was Jessica and she was running toward the ocean.

Lights began snapping on in other windows. Knocking his tea to the floor, Barker jumped from his chair, darted down the stairs and headed toward the screaming figure that disappeared into the darkness.

Barker caught up to her at the edge of the beach. She had stopped running and was just standing there weaving back and forth and keening, like a woman who's just been told her fisherman husband won't be coming home from the sea.

Barker grabbed her by the shoulders and she slumped against him so he had to hug her to keep her from collapsing entirely. "Jess," he said, "what is it?"

She was racked by a series of moist sobs and Barker started her back toward the buildings, she half walking and he half dragging her. Others were running to meet them now. Harris got there first, followed by Merrill, then Ian Snell. It struck Barker funny how a woman screaming brought the men out. It must be some primal thing that stirred in them, perhaps enhanced by eating meat seared over an open fire not two hours before.

They started to take her back inside, but Betty Snell met them in the doorway and shook her head. "Not here," she said. So they lifted her up the stairs to the Snells' on the second floor. Betty followed and the men left her with a still sobbing Jessica and went back downstairs.

Jeremy Smith lay on the floor, blood in a puddle around him and splattered on the walls and furniture. He was without a shirt, and there were puncture marks on his back where someone had driven something into him repeatedly and violently.

Ian Snell grabbed a blanket off the chesterfield and tossed it over the body.

Harris almost made to grab it back, then stopped and simply muttered, "Jesus, the carpet's already ruined. Did you have to use up a perfectly good blanket, too?"

Snell didn't hear him. He was on the phone to the police.

The cops got there fast. They took control of the crime scene and then, as soon as the Medical Examiner pronounced Jeremy Smith dead, the forensic crew went to work crawling around with vacuum cleaners and toothbrushes like Molly Maids bucking for a promotion. They dusted everywhere for latent prints and studied the splatter marks on the walls and the floor like fortune tellers gawking at tea leaves.

Barker was standing outside, apart from the rest of the guests who milled around talking nervously among themselves. He was looking at the sky again, hunting for constellations.

A man in a well tailored suit came walking toward him.

"Find anything?" he asked.

"Excuse me?" Barker replied.

The man pointed into the air. "Up there. Find any constellations?"

Barker shrugged. "Just the Dipper," he said. "And I think maybe Orion."

"Not yet," the man said. "Only see Orion in the wintertime." He looked up at the sky in silence for several seconds, and then he turned fully to Barker. "My name's Tyler. I'm in charge of this investigation." He flashed a shield in front of Barker's face but it was too dark to read it.

"Ask away."

"You knew the deceased?"

"We've been down here at the same time for the last five years."

"Ever since Mr. Harris bought Oceanview?"

"That's right."

"Can you think of any reason why someone would want to kill Jeremy Smith?"

Barker shook his head. "No."

"I understand Harris and the deceased had an argument earlier today."

Barker wondered who he'd heard that from. "People have arguments all the time."

Tyler ignored that. "Do you know what it was about?"

"It was about money. Harris wanted Jeremy to refinance Oceanview and Jeremy refused."

"They'd had this conversation before?"

"Yes."

The questions continued for about ten minutes, Tyler flipped his notebook closed, thanked Barker and moved away. Barker went inside and was in the kitchen making tea when he saw the body come out of the Smiths', carted by two ambulance attendants. Then the Medical Examiner came out followed by the cops, and they all drove away.

As they pulled out of the parking lot, there was a knock at Barker's door. It was Ian Snell.

"Jessica's okay," he said. "Betty gave her something to calm her down and she's sleeping. Betty'll stay with her, and when she wakes up we'll see if she needs any more attention."

Barker nodded. "If there's anything I can do."

"Not at the moment." He opened Barker's fridge and took out a Miller. "I had an interesting chat with the guy they use as a Medical Examiner."

"Uh huh."

"Yep, he's a local doctor they use on cases like this. For heavy-duty forensic stuff they send up to Boston, but he can pronounce death and do basic autopsies and things like that. He gave me a look at the body. A lot of wounds. We counted about twenty-seven, a good dozen of them post mortem."

"Did they find the knife?"

"Wasn't a knife. Most of the wounds were round, like the killer used a skewer or something. But there are a few that didn't penetrate very deep, mostly the post mortem ones so maybe the killer was getting tired or something, and they aren't round. They look more square. Like maybe he used two instruments. Put one down, picked the other one up. We'll know more when the stuff comes back from Boston. Anyway, whatever the murder weapon was, they didn't find it." He drained the beer and slapped the empty down on the counter. "Thanks. I'll keep you posted."

∽

Barker had just walked out of a shoe store on the main street in Hyannis with a new pair of Rockports under his arm when he saw Snell and the local ME shake hands and go their separate ways.

"Hi," Barker said. "Any update?"

Snell smiled and shook his head. "Not much. And they haven't exactly moved very far forward on tracking down the murder weapon. They have a room full of forensic experts up in Boston stabbing pot roasts with any pointed object they can get their hands on. No match yet."

"They'll turn something up eventually."

"I think what's partially driving them nuts is that they've picked up some microscopic metal fragments that seem to indicate the same weapon made all the wounds."

"So they've got a square peg, round hole problem," Barker chuckled.

Snell nodded. "They just haven't been able to find what they're looking for."

Barker looked thoughtful for a moment and then said, "Maybe that's because they don't know where to look."

"Pardon me?"

"Oh, just thinking out loud. See you back at the place." He turned and walked slowly back towards the ocean.

~

Barker was waiting in the Oceanview parking lot when Snell pulled in.

"Ian," he called. "Come with me. I want to show you something."

They climbed the stairs to Barker's deck and went inside. Barker led the way to the kitchen. A large, thick filet stood on the cutting board.

"Look at this," Barker said.

He picked up something that lay next to the steak and, holding it like a knife, he stabbed it into the meat and pulled it out again, the raw meat sucking at the blade as it withdrew. It left a neat, round puncture.

"Now, look at this."

Carefully, he pressed the same instrument about a quarter of an inch into the beef and took it away. The hole was square.

Snell whistled. "What is that?" he asked.

Barker held it up so Snell could see. It looked like every other screwdriver he'd ever seen, except that the head of it was square. "It's called a Robertson screwdriver," Barker said. "They use them all over the place in Canada. I borrowed this one from Merrill. They come in four or five different sizes and I bet if the cops are put onto it they'll find a match pretty quick."

Snell took the screwdriver from Barker and studied it carefully. "Learn something new every day. So are you going to educate the cops now?"

"Why don't you tell your buddy the ME? Let him be a hero."

~

They arrested Harris around three o'clock that afternoon. Barker watched from the deck as Harris's door opened and he came out in handcuffs, escorted by Tyler and two officers in the blues of the Barnstable police.

They put him in the back of a squad car and drove slowly out of the lot.

The phone call came half an hour later. Harris sounded calm but intense. "I need you, pal. Come as soon as you can."

Barker was patted down before they let him in, then he and Harris sat across a small table from one another on moulded plastic chairs. A cop with a large pistol in an open holster stood by the door.

"I'm scared," Harris said. "You gotta do a couple things for me."

"Anything."

"I need a lawyer. All I know around here are a couple of real estate guys, and I don't want somebody court appointed. I want the best there is."

"Did you do it?"

"How stupid do you think I am? Get me someone from Boston or something. Somebody good. Get me whoever the Kennedys use." His shoulders drooped suddenly and his head fell forward. "Just get me out of here."

"What are you gonna use for dough?" Barker asked. "I mean, I can lend you a few bucks but..."

"Thanks, but I don't want to borrow your money."

"Then take a court appointee."

"God damn it, I don't want some second-rate jerk who passed law school with a C minus. Do they have the death penalty in this state? Get me someone good. I'll pay somehow."

"How, for Christ sake?"

Harris didn't answer for more than a minute, then he said quietly, "I'll sell the place."

"Aw, Jesus," Barker said, "there has to be another way."

"You tell me what it is."

"A bank?"

"They wouldn't loan me a penny to fix the place. You think some lard-ass banker is going to loan me big bucks to hire a lawyer to defend me on a charge of killing another lard-ass banker? Gimme a break. Look, call my real estate agent and get her looking for a buyer."

Barker looked thoughtful, then said simply, "I'll buy it."

"Huh?"

"I'll buy it. Then when you get kicked loose from here the place'll still be there. I'll work up an offer today. After I call some Boston lawyers."

Harris's eyes welled up. "Thanks," he said. "Bring the offer as soon as you can. Now please get me a lawyer. Jesus, I'm scared."

∽

After leaving Harris, Barker had called a friend of his at a Boston agency and got the names of several key attorneys. One of them was sitting in that little room with Harris right now, mapping out a defense.

Then Barker had called a real estate lawyer in Hyannis and had an offer prepared. He'd deliver it to Harris later on. Finally, he'd called back to Toronto to start the arrangements for selling his house and arranging the rest of the necessary financing.

It didn't look good for Harris, now that the cops knew what the murder weapon was. They knew one just like it was missing from Merrill's kit. They knew about Harris's financial situation. They knew about his violent argument with Jeremy Smith. It may or may not have been enough to convict him, but either way the decision could be a long time coming.

Now, Barker sat on the deck in the sunshine. A cold bottle of Miller stood open on the wooden railing next to his feet. The sky was clear and the sun sparkled on the water. He raised his glass in a toast and said, aloud but softly, "Well, Barker, think you'll do well in the resort game?"

"No idea," he answered himself. "But I'm certainly willing to take a stab at it."

He laughed loudly at that and looked down at the sea wall where Jessica sat, the soft wind caressing her golden hair.

Dents

Sabrina was halfway across the street by the time Kay stepped off the curb. Typically, Sabrina had given a cursory glance to the right, determined that no traffic was coming along the five-lane, one-way street, and started across. Kay, on the other hand, took long and careful looks, first to the right, then the left. She checked for any other streets, alleys or parking lots nearby from which a car could unexpectedly emerge. Once she was completely satisfied, she started across.

"Hurry," Sabrina said, reaching the far side and turning to look back. "We're late already."

"I'm coming," Kay said as she stepped up onto the sidewalk next to her niece. "It's just that I'm careful."

"I don't know why you always look around so much before you cross that street. It's one way. Nobody'll be going that way." She made a sweeping gesture with her arm, indicating a direction against the normal flow of traffic. Somewhere out of sight a light had changed and cars now streamed past, all in the same eastbound direction, clogging all five lanes.

Kay shook her head. "That's what Sidney always used to tell me, too, and look what happened to him. You really should take more care yourself."

"What happened to Uncle Sidney," Sabrina said, "was a stupid fluke. Somebody turning the wrong way onto the street like that. Never happen again in a million years." She looked at her watch and muttered, "Oh, dear, look at the time." She moved off again quickly, setting a pace Kay could not match. Watching the articulated roll of Sabrina's behind as she moved, Kay recalled other women she'd known who walked like that. It was in no way strange that trouble always seemed to follow them.

∽

"Take your time, Mrs. Underhill, and read everything. You can use an empty office if you'd like more privacy."

Kay looked at the sheaf of papers stacked up on the lawyer's desk. The right hand edges bristled with yellow self-adhesive stickers reading "Please sign and date here". Kay shook her head and took the pen he offered her.

"Oh, it's all right," she said. "I probably wouldn't understand it anyway." She gave him her most grandmotherly smile. "And, please, I know you young people are much less formal than we used to be. Call me Kay."

Bigelow nodded in understanding and turned the pages for her as she signed, peeling off the stickers and crumpling them in his hand. When she was finished, Bigelow shuffled the pages into a neat pile and set them back on the desk. "Thank you very much for coming in, Kay. This has been most helpful. Can I arrange for someone to drive you home, or is Sabrina taking you?"

Kay shook her head. "Oh no. I have a couple of errands to do and then I'll walk to the subway. Sabrina has other plans, I'm sure, and it's such a lovely day. Thank you anyway." She gathered up her light spring coat and headed for the door. "Are you riding down in the elevator with me, Sabrina?"

"I'll be a couple more minutes. You go ahead. I want to talk to Mr. Bigelow about trying to find" - she paused and gave Kay a cold-eyed look - "you know who."

Kay knew only too well. Sabrina's husband Earl had abandoned her the previous year. Their marriage had been old fashioned in the way that Earl kept control of the finances, keeping his wife in the dark as to how the money was spent and how much of it there was. Or, in this case, how little. He disappeared one day, leaving behind very little trace of his ever having been there, except for the lengthy string of creditors and lawyers whose letters and phone calls and bulky legal documents arrived at her door almost daily. In the end, she was forced to declare bankruptcy. The bank took the house, and one night someone came and repossessed the car, and the meagre retirement fund that had all been in his name was liquidated and taken away, too. Broke and shattered, she went to live with her only relative, who let her stay free. Kay didn't mind the company, since Sidney was no longer there to lift his feet as he sat reading on the sofa so she could vacuum under them.

"Will you be home in time for supper, Sabrina?"

"Yes, Kay."

"I'll see you then." Kay smiled her goodbyes and shut the door behind her.

As soon as the door clicked into place, Sabrina's shoulders slumped and she leaned against one of Bigelow's guest chairs.

"Are you all right?" he asked in mild alarm. "Sit down, please. Can I get you something? A glass of water? A cup of tea?"

Sabrina shook her head. "I feel terrible about this." She had gone very pale and her lips turned down. Bigelow sat down in the chair next to Sabrina's. One of her hands rested against her forehead, but the other dangled over the arm of the chair and he felt an impulse to take it and hold it gently, wondering if that would comfort her. He resisted, not wanting to be misunderstood.

Instead, he spoke softly to her. "I know this can't be easy for you, Sabrina. But don't be so hard on yourself. You weren't tricking her into giving you title to the house and everything so you could kick her out on the street. You weren't even getting her to commit herself to Bedlam. What you're doing is ultimately for her own good."

"Does that make it right, though? That's the part I can't get around. Do I have the right to do this? And am I just being selfish?"

"Legally, no, you don't have the right. You knew that from the beginning. Are you being selfish? No. Believe me, I've seen selfish people sitting in both these chairs. Squabbling over the spoils of a divorce or the petty details of an inheritance. I know what selfishness and greed look like, and neither of them looks like you." He hadn't intended to say it that way, but Sabrina didn't react to any deeper meaning that might have been implied.

"Why are you helping me like this? You could get in serious trouble."

He looked at her for a second and thought and then told her part of the truth. "My father promised your uncle that this firm would take care of your aunt to the best of our abilities. Dad didn't get more specific than that. So now that he's gone, I have to interpret his meaning as best I can." He smiled at her.

"I'm sorry," she said, as if she hadn't heard. "I'm having trouble concentrating. What did she sign again?" Bigelow rose and stepped to the desk, picking up the papers and offered them to Sabrina who shook her head. "No. You'd only have to explain them to me anyway. Just tell me."

Putting the documents down again, Bigelow perched on the edge of the desk. "There was a whole bunch of things. A release form for the harvesting of vital organs for transplant, for example. Not very common in women her age, but we needed some red herrings. The one thing she signed that was important is just a kind of power of attorney. It gives you the right to take over her finances any time, if it looks like she's starting to make irrational decisions. Ones that could end up harming her, or someone else. You may end up in court over it, but with some of the things you've told me she's talked about doing, the trips and the purchases, I can't think of many judges who wouldn't see it your way right down the line. To be honest, we handle her money to such a degree already that it'll probably never come up. But it lets you protect your aunt. And your own future after she's gone."

" Is this a terrible thing?" she asked quietly.

"No," he said, bending forward to touch her on the arm, just below the elbow.

∽

The day had grown warmer in the short time Kay had been in Bigelow's office. She had emerged from the elevator wearing her coat, but after a few minutes outside she took it off and tucked it over the crook of the arm that held her purse. What she really felt like doing was crumpling the collar in her right hand and flinging the coat over her shoulder, walking with it dangling down her back the way Sidney always used to, but that didn't seem to be something women of her age did. Sidney certainly wouldn't have approved. But maybe one day she would do it anyway.

Walking along with her coat draped over her bent arm, Kay found herself thinking of her life since Sidney had been killed. She sometimes felt guilty that she didn't miss him more, and often on a pleasant Sunday afternoon she would visit his grave, placing a small pebble on the headstone to indicate that she had been there. She would occasionally bend to pluck a weed from the grass that flourished above him, and talk to him about the fact that she didn't miss him too much. Sometimes she would feel a dull, quiet longing. Sometimes she would come into the house, for an instant forgetting that he was dead, and expect to hear him stomping across the hardwood floors, but those moments were growing steadily fewer and never lasted long. And though she would apologize to Sidney, she knew in her heart that she didn't really mean it.

Her first stop after the lawyer was a car dealership. She had been there several times already, and most of the salesmen smiled when she walked in. Her car stood glistening in the centre of the showroom floor. Sleek and seductive and red. Its top down. Beckoning.

ↄ

"Do you know what she's thinking of doing now?" Sabrina was standing with her back to the sun streaming in through the window, her features obscured by shadow.

"What?" Bigelow asked.

"She's thinking of buying a car."

Bigelow shrugged. "Really? What about the Rambler?"

"She doesn't like it. She wants to get rid of it. She's thinking of getting a sports car. An Alfa Romeo, I think she said."

"A sports car? You mean like a little two-seater, two-door, gear shift, no trunk space kind of thing?"

"That's what she's talking about."

"Oh, my. That's not cheap. It could put quite a dent in her reserves."

"But it's not even the money so much. Why would a woman her age want a car like that? I don't even know how she'll get in and out of it without help."

Bigelow considered that in silence, watching Sabrina in the sunlight and picturing, for an instant, the two of them in what he imagined an Alfa Romeo to look like. Her hands on the wheel. Her hair in the wind.

"I really don't know what she's thinking," she said, turning her back to him and watching the afternoon through glass.

෴

Sidney hadn't left Kay as wealthy as some women her age. The house had been paid for years ago and, like most real estate in Toronto, had soared in value, but she wasn't nearly ready to sell that. She liked living on her own. And now, with Sabrina there to do many of the chores for her, it was easier. Other than that, there were the proceeds from the painting business that had not fetched as high a price as she had hoped, and there were Sidney's few cautious investments, overseen by Bigelow's firm, that paid off modestly.

Kay was wise enough to understand that, at her age, robust health was a fickle thing. One tumble on an icy sidewalk could rob her of that forever. She was not, however, content to coddle herself. It was her intention to get the most out of her remaining life. There were trips she wanted to take, things in life she now had the opportunity to experience. There was no longer the option of delay. She would use her money on herself, on spending her years exactly as she chose.

This, Kay suspected, did not fit in with Sabrina's image of the future. Kay had seen the look on her niece's face when Kay announced that she was flying first class to London, staying in a suite at the Strand for a week, hiring a car and driver, and going to the theatre.

Kay knew that Sabrina, being her only living relative, wanted her aunt to live as frugally as possible for as short a time as possible, so she could inherit all that was left. Kay hated to disappoint family but, as she well knew, life was full of disappointments. No one's life ever turned out quite the way one might have wished or expected.

She was almost ready for the car. She would trade in her old, boxy Plymouth, pack a couple of bags, and drive north. She had always wanted to visit the Yukon, and Whitehorse would be her first destination.

Closing her eyes, the passing traffic buzzing in her ears, Kay imagined the feeling. Rocketing up the Alaska Highway with the ragtop down. The pure, crisp wind sharp in her nostrils, grabbing and wrestling with her hair. Steel grey and straight, as if it were ironed every morning, Kay's shoulder-length hair was combed back from her high forehead. She refused to put it up or perm it or have it rinsed blue like so many other women. Sidney had loved her hair, gripping it so passionately it hurt when they were in bed together.

"Are you all right?"

Kay opened her eyes, disoriented by having to pull herself back from the tundra so abruptly. A middle-aged woman was standing a few feet away, staring at Kay with concern. "Are you all right?" she asked again.

Kay looked around, assuming the woman could not be talking to her. But there was no one else near. "Why, yes," Kay said slowly, confused by the woman's distress.

"Do you know where you're going? How to get home? Is there someone I can call?"

It registered then. An old woman, standing in blissful oblivion of the tumult around her, eyes closed, perhaps weaving slightly as she dreamed of freedom. She probably looked lost or deranged to someone who expected helplessness in the elderly. Kay laughed and shook her head. "Of course I know where I'm going," she said, an image of the north flashing like lightning through her mind. In a show of defiance, she crumpled the collar of her coat in her hand and tossed it over her shoulder. Yes, she thought walking away, a convertible is the perfect thing to do.

⁓

"Mr. Bigelow always seems like a very pleasant young man," Kay said to Sabrina over dinner.

"Yes, he's very nice."

"I didn't notice a ring. Is he married?" She gave Sabrina one of the benign smiles she knew her niece found highly irritating. "Perhaps I should invite him for dinner one Saturday night."

"I don't think that's a good idea, Kay." Sabrina set her fork down on her plate. She knew what was coming.

Kay put on a look of surprise. "I'm sorry. I didn't mean to meddle. It's just, he's young and attractive." She paused, than added sweetly, "And we both know lawyers make a lot of money."

"Kay, please don't."

"Whatever do you mean? My dear, it's just that I know what it is to lose a husband - although mine didn't abandon me - and a young woman like you should have a man in her life. Preferably a man with money."

"Excuse me, please." Sabrina gathered up her dishes and left the table. Kay continued eating, smiling to herself when she heard the water running in the kitchen sink as her niece began the washing up.

⁓

When Kay turned eighteen, her father had bought her a car. It was a second-hand convertible roadster, and she drove it with exuberance. She revelled in the freedom it gave her and the speeds at which it would take her. Through the Depression, she hoarded what little money she had and spent most of it on gasoline. When she first met Sidney, she drove them to dances and parties two or three times. But he accused her of being reckless and driving too fast, and soon he took on the driving himself anytime they were together. Reluctantly, she let him. But whenever she was alone she drove with abandon, the long silk scarf she wore trailing behind her like Isadora.

For the longest time, she drove convertibles. She remembered her cars fondly and vividly. The 1952 Studebaker Hawk. The 1966 Parisienne. And then came the boxes. As Sidney got older he became more and more concerned with safety. He would not allow any more convertibles, insisting instead on sedans. He drove increasingly slowly and cautiously, hunching tensely over the steering wheel. His dislike for driving, always strong, grew with fierce intensity. Yet he still would not drive with Kay. Often he hid the car keys in places she could not find them.

From the very first time she drove, Kay had always felt perfectly at home behind the wheel. Driving with her left elbow resting on the top of the door in a way her father and Sidney both frequently informed her was not ladylike.

ς

"We may actually have some news about your husband," Bigelow said.

Sabrina shut her eyes and clenched the phone.

Bigelow could hear her ragged breathing, but he said anyway, "Sabrina, are you there?"

"I'm here." Her voice was faint and battered. "What have you found out?"

"Well," Bigelow said, "he's turned up in Calgary, so the fact that he hasn't left the country makes it easier. He's working. And as far as I know he has no idea that we've dug him up. Now we only need to see what's possible."

"I just need help to get back on my feet. Every penny is going to pay off somebody. And it's always money that he owed."

"We'll do everything we possibly can." He spoke gently. "Could you come in tomorrow afternoon at three? I can give you more details about what we know and about what you can realistically hope for. In the meantime, if you need money..." He let the sentence hang, but she had heard the end of it before. He had offered to help her financially on several occasions, but she wanted to make her own way. Get free of the legacy of Earl once and for all and start again. Trying something different this time.

～

Longevity ran in Kay's family. All her grandparents had lived well past ninety, one grandmother surviving to a hundred and three. Sabrina's mother, Kay's younger sister, was Kay's only relative to die young, slipping in the bathtub at sixty-two and fracturing her skull on the edge of the sink as she fell. Sabrina sometimes grew frightened that she would never be free of debt and that she would have to live with Kay forever. And Kay, distracted and disoriented as she often seemed, would never slip and would never die.

"What time are you meeting Mr. Bigelow, again?" Kay asked.

It was the third or fourth time that Kay had asked. "Three o'clock, Kay. I'll be home in time for dinner. Is there anything you'd like me to pick up for you?"

"No, no. I'm going out this afternoon myself. I have a few errands to run. I'll see you later."

Even on the worst days, Sabrina had never wanted Kay to die. But as she walked to the bus stop, Sabrina imagined her aunt leaving the house one day and drifting aimlessly away, never to be seen again.

～

Sidney had never blamed Kay directly for their childlessness, but in her mind she could see his pointed finger. Instead of children, they had the business. It was never wildly successful. Sidney was too withdrawn for that. He lacked fire and drive, and Kay could not ignite it in him. He complained about the stupidity and carelessness of their customers. And she always felt that they sensed his disapproval when they came in. Sidney rarely smiled.

She started out doing the book-keeping and learned everything she could about the business. She began dealing with customers, who appreciated her friendliness and warmth. Eventually she began helping Sidney out on small painting jobs. Sensing often that the customers were happier with her work than with his.

☙

Sabrina took the bus to the subway, took the subway downtown and then a streetcar eastbound for several minutes. It let her off three blocks north of Bigelow's office.

She didn't really like this part of town. Bigelow's building was in the east end of the downtown area, on the south side of a one-way, five-lane eastbound street that was clogged during rush hour but sparsely used the rest of the day. For a stretch of several blocks there were no stores. No restaurants. Hardly ever any pedestrian traffic. Just low-rise offices and warehouses and some film and recording studios. It always made Sabrina slightly nervous, even in the brightness of mid-afternoon.

Concealed from Sabrina's view in a one-lane alley, Kay watched Sabrina approach the curb and do exactly as she always did. Pause at the edge of the sidewalk, look only to the right, and step onto the road. Kay watched the movement of her niece's hips again and understood that Bigelow was drawn to her. That the two of them had schemed to keep Kay from living life as she chose. But Kay was no longer content to live on someone else's terms. She moved forward slightly.

Sabrina had crossed two lanes, was just passing the second strip of broken white lines, when she sensed that something wasn't right. She slowed uncertainly and looked to the right again, but the traffic light that was hidden from view around the bend was obviously still red, holding back any possible oncoming traffic. There were no cars at all in that direction.

Kay checked to make sure there were no police in sight or other idle spectators, then turned out of the alley and aimed the car at her niece.

Sabrina took another step or two, moving closer to the middle of the broad black street. Then, for some unknown reason, she turned and looked to her left.

It took a second to register that the car heading towards her should not have been moving in the direction it was.

When Sabrina paused, like an animal sensing danger and sniffing the air, Kay sped up. When Sabrina turned and saw the car, Kay pressed the pedal to the floor. When Sabrina's eyes locked on hers, and her mouth opened to yell or to scream, Kay smiled and gave a small wave.

Kay watched her niece get closer and closer, her arms held out as if she could stop the vehicle and hold it back, then the car overwhelmed her and bent her double and pulled her from view.

Kay felt the collision right through her. Sabrina must have been more solidly built than she appeared. Kay could feel her niece being dragged by the car, beneath it or to the side. She felt the body thumping on the road and the occasional lurch as the right wheels bounced over something solid. After almost half a block, Kay knew she had to get out of the way. Jiggling the wheel harshly, she shook Sabrina loose, made a sharp turn onto a side street and drove away.

As she drove home, Kay shook her head in disgust. Sidney had been an old man when he died, but at least he'd tried to get out of the way. Sabrina was young and her legs, which Kay felt she'd shown off at the least provocation, were strong and healthy. But she'd just stood there like a deer frozen by headlights, waiting to get hit.

Kay felt despair for young people, if that was how they all reacted in an extreme situation.

Kay drove home without incident. She pulled the car into the garage, climbed out, switched on the overhead light and shut the door behind her. Bending down, she surveyed the damage. There was a large dent in the right front quarter panel, a cracked headlight and some discoloration along the chrome bumper. It would have been easy to fix the damage and touch up the paint. But she decided to redo the entire car. Just in case someone had seen her.

As she prepared for work, she thought of Sidney and how the more he worked on crushed and damaged cars the more he swore about the stupidity of drivers. "Damn people," he used to mutter like a mantra. "Damn people drive too damn fast." And the more afraid he became of driving himself. Kay had never looked at it that way. Every day she was not behind the wheel, her desire to drive grew stronger.

For sentimental reasons, she had kept some of the tools she and Sidney had used in the business. She would repaint the entire car, wait a month or so for the furor to die down, then trade it in on her new convertible. She stood looking at the metallic blue and thought about the colour to use.

Black, she finally decided. Out of respect for the dead.

Trophy Hunter

I want you to find my new wife, Mr. Daniher."

The little cash registers in Milo's head started ringing as soon as the rich man spoke.

"I want you to find my new wife."

Milo didn't have to be a detective to know the guy was rich. He knew it the minute he got the address over the phone. He had it reconfirmed as soon as he saw the house. And when the door opened and he saw Cross standing there he had unassailable proof. Milo recognized the face from countless newspaper and magazine photo ops. And he knew all the stories about the various businesses Cross owned or was reputed to own.

"Find my new wife."

Milo had worked for rich people before and he knew immediately how this job was going to go. If there was one thing Milo prided himself on, it was knowing how other people's clocks were wound. And he knew that this would be the kind of job he had come to treasure. Not hard. Not dangerous. Pushing yourself definitely not required. And at the end, a major payday. It meant he could write his own ticket. It meant clearing enough to cover the cost of life for a few months and then taking Cara to Jamaica for a week, or to Vegas or the Bahamas. And he knew how appreciative she could be on the rare occasions when he took her away somewhere.

"My new wife."

A lot can happen to a wife. She could have been kidnapped and the rich man was scared to go to the cops. He liked press, but not that kind. She could have wandered off from the old folks' home in nothing but a bathrobe and furry slippers. She could have split for Niagara Falls with the delivery guy from the drug store. He called her his new wife, so maybe she got disappointed that he couldn't hold up his end in bed, or maybe she didn't like the fact that it was up all the time. Milo didn't know whether it was one of those or something else entirely, but he didn't much care. Because he did know one thing for sure. He knew how to work this.

How it worked was like this: Milo sets it up about how tough it is to track somebody all by yourself in a city of three and a half million people. He'll do his best but it'll take time. And if somebody doesn't want to be found at all, well, it's a big, wide world out there. Then, having set the stage, Milo hits the rich man for a big day rate, takes a couple of weeks up front as retainer, then fucks the dog. Looks a bit, calls in every couple of days to update on nothing. Every so often he picks up a couple of receipts and floats them past the rich guy's nose as expenses. After a month or so he calls it a day, packs a suitcase, and takes Cara somewhere she can get an all-over tan.

"Do you have a picture of her?" Milo asked.

"No." Cross sounded surprised. "I'm afraid I don't."

Now that was odd. Not many people don't have a picture of the person they're married to. At least, not many people who care enough to hire a private detective to track down a wife who's gone missing. Oh well, Milo thought, maybe she's got some weird phobia. Maybe she's just ugly as homemade sin. Maybe she's from some tribe somewhere that thinks cameras steal your soul. Doesn't matter. Fact is, it made things better. Without a picture to show around he could make the case that the job'd be that much tougher, take him that much longer. Make him that much richer.

"Can you describe her to me, then?" Milo reached in his pocket for a chewed up pen and a half-used note pad.

"Well." Cross sat back, looking up at the ceiling as if fixing an image in his mind. "I can definitely do that, Mr. Daniher. She is between twenty-four and twenty-six years old. She weighs between one hundred fifteen and one hundred twenty-five pounds. She has shoulder length hair, wavy but not curly, some shade of brown, but definitely not blonde. She has long legs and neither tattoos nor pierced body parts, except her ear lobes. She stands between five feet six and five feet eight inches tall."

Milo stopped writing. He knew that a lot of women kept their age secret, and some outright lied about it, so there had to be husbands who didn't know exactly how old their wives were. He knew that everyone's weight fluctuated. And with the way a lot of women dieted and binged they could roller coaster up and down ten pounds from one week to the next. And hair could change length and colour in the bathroom between halves of a football game. But a person's height tended to be pretty consistent. That's what really threw Milo. It didn't sound like Cross was describing someone he knew. It sounded like he was telling the guy at the dealership what options he wanted on his new 4x4.

"Hold on," Milo said. "Can't you be a little more precise? You don't know how tall your wife is?"

"Not yet." The smile again.

Milo scratched his jaw. "I'm sorry, but you lost me back there."

"What do you mean?"

"I mean, it sounds like you're describing *types* of people, not one in particular. What's going on here?"

"Did I not make make myself clear, Mr. Daniher? I said I want you to find my new wife. The woman I intend to marry. If I'd already met her, I wouldn't need the services of a detective."

Milo blinked hard several times, then dug his little finger into his right ear and shook it. He'd done a lot of things for money in his time. He'd chased away raccoons and stolen garbage bags off ritzy front lawns at two in the morning. He'd videotaped every kind of couple imaginable. He'd dragged runaways back to the families they probably had good reason for leaving in the first place. He'd pissed into empty pickle jars, sitting up nights in his car, waiting for guys who'd skipped on their bondsmen to come up for air. He'd repoed cars and intercepted mail and made harrassing phone calls. But he'd never played matchmaker.

"Let me get this straight. You want to hire me to find you a co-ed you can marry. You don't need me, pal. You need a dating service."

"Oh no, Milo. May I call you Milo?"

Milo figured it didn't matter whether he minded or not. So he just shrugged.

"Well then, Milo, you're quite wrong. I need you very much."

"How so?"

"I want this done discreetly. I don't want my name and personal data keyed into some computer system that spits out dessicated spinsters and blubbery widows with condos in Pompano Beach. I want women who fit my specifications exactly. I want it done with no fuss whatsoever. And I have been told, Milo, that you are nothing if not discreet."

In the end, Milo took the job. He quoted a day rate that was twice what he usually got and Cross slipped him three grand up front. Cash.

"Anything else I should know about your sweetheart?" Milo asked.

"A couple of small things, Milo. Intelligence is not an issue. I want a woman who looks very attractive. I'm not interested in intellectual discussions. There are plenty of people with whom I can have those. Indeed, since her opinion will be neither sought nor appreciated, it would be much better if she didn't have one. Also it would be better - in fact it is a prerequisite - that she not have a family."

Milo's eyebrows went up.

"It's simple, Milo. I'm a very rich man. I make no secret of it. And my friends tend also to be very rich men. Many of them, like me, have taken younger wives. In at least two cases of which I am aware, these wives had families. And members of those families had" - he paused as if searching for the right word - "avaricious tendencies. The situations became very unpleasant. Such unpleasantness is something I am determined to avoid."

"Understood," Milo said. "You're not looking for love then. Good. Because I can find you a chick for the rate we discussed. But love costs extra. Anything else?"

"I think that's everything. I expect to hear from you within a week with a progress report. Within two weeks, I expect to begin meeting candidates. Please be aware that I do not want a cattle call. I haven't the time to waste."

He stood up and ushered Milo out of the room. They walked along the panelled hallway toward the front door.

Milo marveled again at the suit of armour standing guard at the foot of the stairs. A suit of armour with a big double-headed axe in one hand.

"Lovely piece, isn't it?" Cross said. He reached out and touched the blade of the axe with his thumb. "Feel it," he said.

Milo pressed the ball of his thumb against the blade and felt it slice the skin. "Sharp."

"Yes. Someday I must outline for you the provenance of the piece, but I'm sure you're too busy for that now." Then he crossed to a set of double doors and opened them wide. "Before you go, I thought you might be interested in this. My trophy room." It was dark with wood panelling, stone fireplace, leather chairs and severed heads sticking out from the wall. There was a moose, a twelve-point buck, a bear and several animals that Milo was sure were on endangered lists somewhere. There were fish too. Trout and muskie and a big billfish on the far wall. The only area of wall with nothing on it was above the fireplace.

Milo pointed at the open space. "What's going up there? You want something pretty big. What's that mantel? About six feet? That marlin'd look good."

"Yes, it actually was there for a time. It took me seven hours to land off Zihouatanejo. It was a wonderful challenge. But beautiful as it is, it felt too common. I want a more exotic trophy." Then he smiled and showed Milo the door.

～

"I have an idea," Cara said.

"Yeah, what's that?" Lying on his back with his eyes closed, Milo felt like a lizard on a hot rock.

"I'll do it."

"You'll do what?" Cara was not one for doing things for other

201

people unless money changed hands, so Milo got nervous right away.

"I'll marry the rich guy."

"What?" He opened his eyes and turned his head to look at her.

"You heard me. I'll marry him. Then I'll ditch him. And we'll get half of everything. That's how community property works, isn't it?"

Milo had explained the job to her over dinner, and she listened with an unusual amount of interest. When he was finished she got quiet for a time, then laid this at his door. "I'll do it." Like she was saying yeah, she'd pick the milk up on the way home from the hair salon. She was unpredictable. That was one of the things Milo liked best about her.

He didn't concern himself much with most of her inconsistencies. It flashed through his mind that she had told him more than once that she really didn't like men. This didn't exactly jibe with suggesting that she marry someone she'd never met, but then Milo knew that people were seldom simple or consistent.

She got out of bed to dress and Milo studied her. This time with more purpose than just enjoyment. She was exactly what Cross had in mind. The right age. The right colouring. The right height and weight and shape. She was smarter than the person Cross was looking for, but that only meant she was smart enough to play dumb. Milo was just thankful that he'd been able to talk her out of getting her navel pierced on her last birthday. "You have an amazing body," he said.

"Thanks," she said. "I like yours, too."

"I'm serious. I think you look great. I think Cross'll think you look great. But I think you should give this thing some deeper thought," Milo said. Something about the idea didn't sit comfortably in the back of his head.

"I will." She slipped into a pair of jeans and did up her belt. "It's only about the money, Milo. I'm tired of feeling stressed over not having enough money."

"So move in with me." It was the umpteenth time of asking. She was renting a house down in the Beaches and it was eating up too big a chunk of her pay.

She pulled on a shirt that didn't reach her waist and then she stretched, showing him her smooth and flat belly. "I don't think that's a good idea,

Milo. Not yet, anyway."

He thought, but you're ready to move in with some rich guy you've never even talked to. But he kept his mouth shut. Instead, he said, "I just don't want to make this look too easy or too much like a set-up. Leave it with me. I'll make it so it can't fuck up."

"I like a man who takes charge," she said.

⌇

For the next week, Milo pretended to work. He placed ads in the classified sections of several newspapers, giving an anonymous post office box. *Successful, established businessman seeks...early to mid-twenties...no children...send letter and photo...* He knew the ads would most likely turn up nothing. Any candidates who did have potential he could just shitcan.

He took out ads in foreign papers too. In England and Ireland and Australia, for women looking to emigrate to Canada. Women for whom marrying a Canadian was the easiest route. This wasn't what Cross wanted, but Milo had to show some effort and, as he'd explain it, you never knew. You don't ask, you don't get. Bearing in mind Cross's desire for brown hair, Milo also advertised in France and Spain, specifying absolute fluency in English. Although, since Cross didn't seem to care if they never opened their mouths for anything but a blow job, that might not matter.

Occasionally, Milo saw women on the street who were close to the type but, he suspected, not perfect. Sometimes he would follow them and take pictures with a telephoto lens. More useless evidence of his keen efforts.

All this information, including clippings of the various ads, copies of the bills, and some early and unacceptable local responses, were presented to Cross during Milo's first update.

"Surely there's something more personal you can do." Cross sounded irritated.

"I am," Milo said. "I'm asking people all the time. 'Do you know somebody?' Things like that. But you have to be careful. You're not going to make much progress using that approach on someone in a bar. And is that who you'd want anyway?"

"I suppose not."

"No, I figured."

Milo left with a week's extension and another grand in his pocket.

Slowly, the responses from overseas started to trickle in. Most of them were useless, but a couple had potential merit. Those Milo ripped up and threw away. He was amazed by the photos some of them sent him. Several were topless. Some totally naked. A few actually sent pictures of themselves, or women they were palming off as themselves, having sex. Milo put those photos in a special file. After two weeks, it was time to up the stakes a notch.

He went to see Cross again, bringing the next batch of mailed-in replies, plus some of his telephoto shots. Included in the pictures he'd taken himself were three women who he was going to have Cross meet. Before he got to meet the woman of his dreams.

Going through the options with Cross, Milo pushed the three ringers hard. They had the look, he pointed out. They didn't have families. At least, none that he'd been able to dig up so far. And he was sure he could interest them in the proposition. Cross bit. Bring them in. Tuesday night. One at eight. One at eight-fifteen. One at eight-thirty. Cross didn't say it in a way that gave Milo the feeling he could negotiate.

One of the three was an acquaintance of Milo. A friend who did amateur theatricals and was close to Cross's description. The others were friends of hers. They all were active in little theatre and wanted to try out their skills in a real life drama. Milo hired them all for a modest sum. Then he sketched the details. Just enough so they'd know what to do. Not enough that they'd screw the deal.

Tuesday at quarter to eight, he met the first potential Mrs. Cross at the front door. She was perky, with an athletic build and auburn hair. Milo escorted her to the trophy room. "Everything'll go fine," he said. "Piece of cake." There was a fire burning in the hearth that accentuated the wall above the mantel. "This is Janet," Milo said.

Cross was sitting in a wing chair, angled slightly away from the fireplace. He looked at the woman carefully, then motioned for her to turn around. "Tell me something about yourself, Janet."

"Like what?"

"Anything at all. About your childhood."

She thought for a moment and then started talking enthusiastically about the pets she'd had, the cottage she'd loved to visit with her family each summer, the friends she'd shared secrets with. Cross shut his eyes while she spoke and gave Milo the impression that he wasn't so much listening to what she said as to the quality of her voice. She was in the middle of a story about a rabbit she'd been particularly fond of when Cross opened his eyes again and interrupted her, "That's enough."

She looked startled, but stopped talking.

"Now," Cross said, "take off your clothes."

Leaning back against the wall by the door, Milo's pulse quickened. He hadn't anticipated this, although it made sense, given what Cross was looking for. He hadn't prepared any of the women for it. This was going to be more interesting than he'd figured.

"Pardon me?" Janet said.

"You heard me," Cross said softly. "Remove your clothes. How you look nude is a significant part of my decision." He looked at her evenly, but Janet didn't reach for button or zipper. Instead she turned, picked up her purse and overcoat from the love seat, gave Milo a hurt and angry look, and left.

"Clearly," Cross said, "she won't do."

"Probably won't do much of anything," Milo joked, but Cross didn't even smile.

The next one worked better. Her name was Mary and when the request was made she didn't hesitate. She simply dropped her clothes in a pile on the floor and turned slowly so that Cross could see her fully. As she faced Milo she winked and stuck out her tongue. "Want me to bend over?" she asked Cross over her shoulder.

Mary's undoing was a small rose tattooed on her behind. As soon as Cross saw it, he said, "Get dressed. You won't do."

"Your loss, my friend," she said as she went through the door.

At Milo's suggestion, the third candidate had become a brunette two days before. She had no tattoos and taking off her clothes was not a problem. But Cross felt her thighs were too heavy and she, too, was sent home.

"So far, Milo, I'm less than impressed."

It became clear to Milo that Cross had been spun along as far as possible. It was time the rich guy got to know Cara.

"Mr. Cross," Milo said over the phone the next day, "I think we have a strong contender."

"Tell me," Cross said.

The meeting with Cross went just the way Milo figured it would. He got there a couple of minutes before eight. Cross was never on time, but Milo knew that he got mad as hell if you weren't there when you were supposed to be.

He waited in the library. It was packed with books, floor to ceiling, on dark wooden shelves that covered almost every inch of wall. Once, Milo had made the mistake of taking a book off the shelf. It was selected works of Milton, beautifully bound and quite old. Milo was reading *Samson Agonistes* aloud when Cross came into the room.

"Don't ever touch my books," Cross said, taking the volume from Milo's hand.

"It's Milton," Milo said, but Cross was not impressed by Milo's taste in literature.

"Don't ever touch anything that belongs to me," Cross said. Then he smiled and offered Milo a coffee.

That's how Milo learned. He never touched anything, never sat down or opened a door, unless the rich man told him to. The last thing he wanted to do was fuck up the deal.

Cross motioned for Milo to come into the trophy room. The space above the fireplace was still vacant, Milo noticed. Cross was taking his time deciding what to put there. Maybe he had a trip to Africa coming up, or Borneo, and he was waiting to see what he bagged while on safari.

Milo sensed that Cross was impatient. He didn't sit down himself. He didn't motion for Milo to sit either. He just held out his hand for the photographs. Milo handed them over.

Cross flipped through them once quickly, then a second time, studying each one at length. They were a mixed bag of images. Some candid shots of Cara walking along the street or sitting at outdoor cafes. Some were studio shots. They were all pretty wholesome, a couple just bordering on cheesy. But he knew by now what the rich guy went for. He didn't like aggressive women. He didn't want one who would look him in the eye and ask him, "Do you want to fuck?" Cara could play it both ways.

Milo figured Cross liked what he saw. "Bring her here. Tomorrow night. This same time."

And then Milo was outside, heading for his car.

$\backsim$

It was all turning real. Milo took a long route home, doubling back on himself and circling like a hawk. His mind was cranking all the way. Here it was. If he shut his eyes he could almost smell the money, almost feel how different life would be to the touch. It would feel like silk and chenille and twenty-year-old malts. But that wasn't all he thought about. He worried too. This was not unusual and it wasn't necessarily bad either. Milo worried about a lot of things. He sweated the details. That's why things worked out so well for him all the time. That's why this thing was going so smooth. Had been ever since Cara suggested it and Milo cooked up the scheme. But whenever he thought about Cara being involved in it right up to her tender neck, he had mixed feelings.

Of course, he had mixed feelings about Cara most of the time. He wasn't in a position to say forget it. Forget the money. Let's walk away while we can. No, much as he thought about it he couldn't bring himself to make that big a sacrifice. On the other hand, he couldn't tell her that he'd stick around after she'd taken half the rich guy's dough. He couldn't make that promise. He'd be just as likely to take his cut and head for greener pastures.

He loved her, or thought he did. He certainly liked the way her body looked and the way she moved it. But he hated the fact that she was secretive. He was good at laying secrets bare most of the time. But he couldn't dig far into her.

He knew the facts that she'd given him. But he also knew that it was far from everything. It was like her life was a panoramic photograph that she had carefully cropped down to wallet size and given to him. This is what he knew:

She never talked about her childhood. The story she told Milo started when she was fourteen and doing a lot of drugs. She smoked a plantation's worth of grass and hash and dropped acid. Nothing heavy, she said. Nothing in the vein. She left home when she was seventeen. She got an apartment with a friend and began a series of nothing jobs she didn't like. Often, she dropped them at a moment's notice, going out for lunch and simply not going back. At nineteen she married a guy she claimed she didn't want to marry and went west with him. They lived for a time in Vancouver, which she loved, then Edmonton, which she hated. She hated the cold and the tedium and the marriage, and she fell into a clinical depression. At some point along the road she told Milo she'd thought about suicide. But he got the sense maybe she'd done more than think.

At another point, she picked up a major case of panic and didn't go outside for months. It lingered still. She wouldn't ride the subway or get on a plane or step into an elevator. She left her husband. Left him, more or less. She still spent one night a week with the guy even after she started going out with someone new. Then she moved in with the new guy. Another thing she claimed she didn't want to do. Eventually, she stopped spending nights with the ex-husband and stayed home most evenings. Until she met Milo. And that was it. Everything else was secret. She even refused to tell him how old she was. But he guessed she was in Cross's range.

He had problems with turning her over to Cross. On the other hand, there was probably more money than he could count. He started for home.

∽

"You ready?"

They were sitting in the car in front of Cross's place. Cara hadn't given away anything when she saw it. "Big," was all she said.

"Wait'll you see the inside."

She said nothing at all to that.

It was about ten to eight. "We still have a few minutes," Milo said. Cara was staring out through the windshield. It wasn't bright in the car, but the security floodlights shining on the property let Milo see enough of her face. She had this look on her that Milo never knew if he was decoding right.

"We don't have to go through with it," he said. He put his hand on top of hers. She didn't pull away, but neither did she respond. "We can just leave." He felt better saying it. Like a responsibility was lifted off him. "We can drive home and I'll tell Cross to forget it. There's lots of money to be had out there. We can pick ours up somewhere else."

Cara shook her head. "No. I can't get out of this now."

"You mean you don't want to."

"I mean I can't." She opened her door. "Let's go," she said. "Get me to the church on time."

Milo followed her to the house.

∽

Inside, Cara stopped for a moment in the foyer and looked around. She took in the vaulted ceiling and the circular staircase and the gilt-framed oil paintings. But all she commented on was the suit of armour. "Look at that," she said and went up to it, reaching out to the blade of the axe.

"Careful," Milo said. "It's sharp."

"I guess you'd want it to be," she said.

Cross didn't say it when he opened the door to let them in, but Milo could tell that he was pleased. Cross was checking Cara out while she checked out the suit of armour. The armour didn't pay any attention.

Then Cross led them into the trophy room.

He told Cara to undress. She did it right away, but mechanically. The mask was still in place. When she was naked, she stood waiting with her arms at her sides.

As Cara waited, Cross lifted a pair of surgical gloves from his desk and put them on. He didn't say anything. Milo didn't say anything. Neither did Cara. The sucking sound of rubber seemed very loud. When the gloves were on, Cross wiggled his fingers. Then he motioned for Cara to turn around.

She did and Cross walked across the carpet and stood very close to her. In the middle of her back was a large mole. Cross reached out with his right hand and pressed it, then bent his index finger back and flicked it hard, like a child shooting a marble. Cara winced and Cross said, "This can be fixed."

Then he grabbed her hair and lifted it up, peering at the skin of her neck. He placed his free hand on the top of her head and twisted it sharply to the left and then to the right. Still holding her hair, he bent her ears forward with his thumb, one then the other. Milo figured he was looking for face lift scars.

Cross seemed satisfied because, without letting go of her hair he stepped around in front of her. "Bend forward," he said, pulling downward. "Not that far." He jerked her head backward and she whimpered.

Milo was starting to feel uncomfortable. "Mr. Cross..."

"It's okay, Milo," Cara said.

"You can leave if you like," Cross said, but Milo didn't move.

When Cara was bent forward at the angle Cross wanted, the rich man started pawing at the top of her head. Pushing her hair around with rough, sharp motions. Looking for dark roots, Milo supposed.

Satisfied with her head, Cross put a hand under Cara's chin and jerked up. "This won't take much longer," he said. But to Milo it seemed to take quite some time.

∽

"Tomorrow at eleven, have her at this address." He handed Milo a card with the name of a well known cosmetic surgeon. "Get him to look at that thing on her back. If he says it can be fixed with no sign, call me right away. If he says there'll be a problem with scarring, call me in two days with other possibilities." Cara was standing near the front door with her coat bunched around her. Her chin was tucked down into the collar and she looked cold. Cross never looked at her.

"Good work, Milo. We're very close with this one." He gave Milo one of his rare smiles. "I expect to hear from you tomorrow," he said.

෭

"Are you all right?"

"Sure." She said it without conviction. Just the way she said it when Milo suggested doing something together other than going to the two or three restaurants she liked.

Milo's feelings of discomfort weren't going away in a hurry. "We don't have to go see that doctor tomorrow," he said. "I don't have to call him."

"I can't get out now," she said. "Take me home. I want a bath."

෭

The plastic surgeon was expecting them. They saw him right on the dot of eleven o'clock. Milo was impressed. Cross must have really had some sway to get a doctor to see you on time. Of course, you paid cash for this type of treatment. It wasn't a health care thing, necessary because of an accident or something. Cash made a difference. Milo knew it. So did Cara.

The doctor seemed very gentle. He told Milo to wait in the reception area, then he asked Cara to go into an examining room and remove her shirt. She would find a gown to wear hanging on the back of the door. He gave her a few minutes while he checked some charts and made a phone call, then he went to the examining room and tapped

211

lightly on the door. "May I come in?"

Milo did not hear Cara's response, but the doctor opened the door and went inside. He was not gone long. He came out, making notes. Cara followed a minute or two later.

"I have to tell you," the doctor said, "that based on a preliminary examination there's no medical reason to remove that mole. Cara, you tell me that it's always been there. It hasn't changed in size or colour or texture - hasn't changed in any way at all. We can do a biopsy, but my feeling is it won't show anything abnormal. Sometimes, to be quite frank, removing a benign growth such as this can trigger cancerous growth."

"Thank you, doctor, but there are other issues here. If you do remove it, will there be any scarring or anything?"

The doctor shook his head. "No, it's a very straightforward procedure. Any mark left behind will be so insignificant as to be unnoticeable. But again I have to tell you that there's no medical reason to do this."

Cara put on her jacket. "It's not being done for medical reasons," she said.

∽

Cross was happy with the news, as far as Milo could tell. The rich man's voice didn't change very much. "This is good. Tell her to be ready tomorrow evening at seven. Have her dressed for a wedding. Not a white gown. I'm not a traditionalist. But something demure and simple. I'll have a car pick her up. She needn't pack anything. Clothes will be arranged."

"You're getting married tomorrow night?"

"Yes. I'm sorry, but it will be a private affair. However, we do have business to conclude. Come and see me now."

As he listened to the phone humming in his ear, Milo's head started to swim. This was moving faster than he'd planned. He wished everything would slow down for a second so he could think.

Until that happened, he had to keep moving at the pace that was set. That or get left behind. He went to see Cross. They met in the trophy room as usual. Milo took a good long look around because he sensed he might never see it again.

Cross handed him a fat envelope. "What's this?" Milo asked. Cross had more than paid up already.

"A bonus. You've outdone yourself. Once that small disfigurement is corrected, she'll be perfect. I assure you that, should any of my friends need the services of a private detective, I'll be sure to recommend you highly." He placed a hand on Milo's back and guided him to the door. "I also trust that I can count on your continued discretion."

"You bet," Milo said. He looked at the space over the mantel again and for the first time an uncomfortable thought crossed his mind. "Good luck finding something for up there."

"Yes," Cross said. Then he laughed. Milo had never heard him do that before.

∽

Almost three weeks and not a word from Cara. Milo knew that most honeymoons were over in a week or two. But he had no idea how long rich-guy honeymoons lasted. Did they go to Europe for the season? Were they on a round-the-world cruise? Were they backpacking in the Andes or spending a month in an ashram getting cleansed? He didn't have a clue.

The evening of the wedding, he'd waited with Cara until Cross's car pulled up out front. She was wearing a short, red, sleeveless dress and a gold chain with her name on it around her right ankle. Her legs looked great and Milo wished she wasn't leaving. Milo wasn't sure the outfit qualified as demure, but that was not his problem.

The driver honked from the street. Cara gave Milo a brief smile and a quick kiss on the cheek. "So long, Milo." He went to hug her, but she'd already turned away, picked up her small purse and taken hold of the door handle.

"Be careful," he said. "Call me and let me know what's happening.

We still have details to work out. And if you want out, any time, all you have to do is phone. Or come see me. I'll haul you out of there in a second."

She smiled at him again and then she left. Through the living room window he saw her walk across the porch, down the steps and out to the car. The driver stood by the door which he shut as soon as she was inside. The car windows were tinted so Milo couldn't tell if she looked back at him or not.

Not a word since. No postcards from the South of France or letters carried by llama down from some Andean retreat.

There were still things they needed to go over. Parts of the plan that had to be worked out now that she was inside. He'd tried to do it before she ever met Cross, but she kept putting him off. Always had a reason. Always told him not to worry, though. They'd work everything out soon.

While he waited for "soon" to arrive, Milo just kept telling himself that he trusted her. He had to. Otherwise, he was fucked.

He took a couple of other cases in the meantime. Some guy wanted to scare a couple of his wetback employees for some undisclosed reason. Milo didn't ask why. He just showed up at the factory pretending to be from Immigration. They got scared enough. He had a couple of beers afterwards and thought about how much he wanted to stop doing this kind of work.

He got passed an insurance claim that the company was sure was bogus. Sometime in the middle of the night he set fire to the guy's shed. It was located at the back of his yard, a good sixty feet from the house. As he watched the man hobble desperately across his yard, hauling a garden hose in his one good arm, Milo figured the claim was legit. But he took pictures. Telephoto. Infrared.

That kind of gig was okay. It paid well enough, though not like Cross. But his heart wasn't in much of anything for those weeks. He missed Cara. And he wondered where the hell she was.

∽

Patience was never Milo's long suit and finally he couldn't wait any more. He had phoned her number at home a couple of times, never expecting her to pick up but just to hear her voice on the answering machine. "You have reached...No one is available to take your call at this time..." He was always amused by the careful enunciation of each word. No endings dropped. Nothing slurred over. He'd hear the message through and then hang up before the beep sounded. Then one day he phoned and, instead of her voice, he got the phone company's. "I'm sorry, the number you have dialled is not in service."

He dialled the number again. Maybe, despite the fact that he'd called it a thousand times, he'd made a mistake. But no. The number was gone. He knew he shouldn't have been shocked. But he felt numb.

He knew there was only one cure. It was time to take charge again.

Milo phoned Cross from a pay phone several blocks from his office. Just in case the rich guy had call display. This time, though, he didn't call Cross's private line - the one that rang only in the trophy room or very softly in the library. He called the general house number. Unlisted, but Milo was a fair to middling detective.

If Cross answered, or the housekeeper, Milo would just hang up. If Cara answered, he'd feel a lot better.

The phone rang three times and then Milo heard a click and "Hello?" Milo caught himself smiling at the sound of her voice.

"Hi, it's me." He realized he was whispering.

"Milo? Why are you calling me?"

That was not the reaction he had anticipated. "Because I miss you every day. And I want to know what's going on. We still have details to work out."

"Details?"

"Yeah." He didn't want to say too much just in case the rich guy was insecure enough to have the phone bugged. "You know, details. About the deal."

"Oh, right."

She didn't sound good. Milo knew something was wrong. "Look, can you get out? Can we meet for dinner or something?"

"Sure," she said. Flat and unenthusiastic.

Milo felt her hesitation and pushed harder. "When? Tonight? To-morrow?"

"I'll have to call you back."

"We have to get together. We have to work out the details. I have to know what's going on."

"I'll tell you," she said. "Just let me do it in my own way."

"You'll call me?"

"Yes, I'll call you."

"When? Tonight?"

"I'll try."

He felt like telling her there was no such thing. She'd either do it because she wanted to or not do it because she didn't. Instead, he softened his voice and tried a gentler tack. "Will you try really hard?"

She made a noise that might have been the least part of a laugh. "Bye," she said and hung up.

She did call him that night, but late. He'd given up. He was lying in bed reading Yeats out loud when the phone rang. He knew it had to be her. He seldom got calls at home. Never at that hour. But even when he picked up the phone and heard her voice it surprised him.

"I can't talk long," she said. "He's in the shower so I've only got a minute. We can have dinner tomorrow night."

"Where?"

She named a restaurant that she liked, where it was quiet and they didn't rush you to get out. "I'll tell you as much as I can then."

"What time?"

"Seven thirty."

"Great," he said. "I love you."

But she was already gone.

⌒

From seven thirty till eight, Milo figured she was tied up. From eight till eight thirty, he figured she'd just forgotten. By quarter to nine he was ready to leave. He was standing with his coat on when she breezed in.

"Sorry," she said but offered no explanation. She wore jeans and a brown leather jacket he'd never seen before.

"That's nice," he said.

"It was a gift." She sat and looked at him, but didn't say anything more.

"So what's the story?" he asked.

"Story?"

Jesus Christ. "Yeah. What's going on? What's your sense of how we play this? How long does he hang on until we can take him? Or does he have some heart condition and maybe he'll kick sometime in the next few months?"

"No," she said, "he definitely doesn't have a heart condition." She laughed, but it was awkward and nervous. "Look, there are some strange things happening, Milo."

No shit. "Strange like what?" he said.

"There's no prenuptial agreement."

Milo had never even considered that. It had never entered his head that Cross would want Cara to sign something before the wedding. He never even considered that his plan might be killed like that, with the stroke of a pen, before it even began. He kicked himself for overlooking something so basic. But, odd that it was that Cross hadn't asked for an agreement, it was a good thing. It meant Milo had dodged the bullet.

"Well, that's good," he said. "Something like that could've really fucked us up."

"It's not good, Milo. It's weird. This guy's got so much money he wipes himself with twenties. And what he's got he hangs on to. Why would he marry a trophy wife and not take every precaution to protect his dough? You read about it all the time, old rich guys getting taken. You told me, he mentioned that kind of thing to you himself. Why wouldn't he protect himself, Milo? Why?"

Milo thought about it but couldn't come up with a reason that made sense. "Maybe he trusts you," he said doubtfully.

"Yeah, right." She looked back over her shoulder, then leaned in halfway across the table. "I don't think he trusts gravity to hold him down. No, I think it's something else. The only thing I can figure is, it's like he knows I'm never going to leave him." She looked back again, as if she were expecting Cross to loom in the doorway any second. "Look, I gotta go. He likes me to stay close to home. That's what he said to me the first day. 'I want to keep you close to hearth and home.' There's something really weird going on."

Milo grabbed her hand across the table. They used to touch fingertips during dinner, but this was different. He grabbed her hand and gripped it tight. "If it's that weird, maybe it's time we got you out of there," he said. "Let's take what we can get now and get you out of there."

She pulled her hand away. "Soon, Milo," she said. "But not yet."

～

The stress was getting to Milo. He went to the gym. He figured he could sweat some of it out. But no matter how hard he pushed himself it didn't help. He kept thinking hard. Something had to be done. He felt like he was losing Cara. She was being sucked away from him by the vaccuum of Cross. That was bugging him plenty. But it wasn't the only thing. There was something Cara had said that was jangling in his brain - way off in the distance like an alarm clock the instant before you wake up.

Milo finally woke up in the shower. He was standing there with the hot water pelting down on the back of his head and neck. The water ran around the sides of his head and poured off his face. His eyes were shut and he played images of Cross and Cara over and over in his head, trying to work it out.

And, for no reason he ever understood, all of a sudden it was clear to him. He opened his eyes and the water streamed over them. "God help me, what have I done?"

As he frantically half-dried himself and dressed, Milo's mind conjured up pictures. He couldn't stop himself. Cross standing in his trophy room. The empty patch of wall above the mantel. Cross asking for a woman with no family. Cross describing the look he wanted. Cara saying he wanted her close to hearth and home. God, that was a sick joke! He wanted something exotic to hang over the fireplace. He wanted a trophy wife. Jesus H. Christ. Milo clenched his teeth to hold down the panic. What have I done? What have I done? Oh God, what have I done?

Outside the gym he found a phone booth. He dropped in a quarter and pounded the keys so hard his finger hurt. As soon as she answered he wanted to scream at her down the phone line, "Get out! Get out now!" But he didn't want to look out of control. Didn't want to make her panic. He stopped himself and breathed in deeply. Well, buddy, he said to himself, you asked for rescue time. Here it is. Don't fuck it up.

The phone rang and Milo thought about what he'd say when she answered. He'd keep his voice calm and tell her that despite what she said, it was time to go. That he was coming for her now. That he'd be there in twenty minutes. The phone rang and rang and Milo would tell her that she didn't need to pack because as soon as he picked her up they were heading for Pearson, and next stop was the nude beach at Negril. The phone rang and rang and rang and Milo slammed the receiver down. Why didn't she answer? He didn't want to consider the possibilities.

Milo left the phone booth and ran to his car. Oh, man, he thought. I'm getting old and stupid. Why didn't I see it?

∽

Just past eight thirty. Milo pulled to the curb a fair distance from Cross's place. He got there early on purpose. To do a recce. To make sure there wasn't something going on he hadn't planned for.

The street was empty. Rich people didn't walk much at night, Milo had noticed. The streetlights were set far apart and the maple trees cast the street and the big houses in shadow. Milo got out of the car and eased the door shut. He was wearing the clothes he usually wore when he worked nights. Black jeans, black canvas high tops, black jacket zippered to the neck. He kept them in a chewed up adidas bag in the trunk in case of emergencies.

He looked around one more time, but nobody was watching that he could see. He started walking to Cross's place. It took him five minutes, and when he got there he could see lights burning on all three floors. Good. Cross was home. That meant maybe nothing had happened to Cara yet. If something had happened, at least Milo wouldn't have to wait to mete out justice.

He went up the flagstone walk and up the stone steps to the big front porch. He'd been in the house often enough to know what was wired and what wasn't. He knew if Cross was inside there'd be no alarm on the front door and the motion detectors would be off. He had no idea how he'd get in. If worse came to worse he could just knock, force his way in, and confront Cross right then and there.

He moved quickly to the door, put his ear to it and listened. He couldn't hear anything inside. He listened longer. Then, before he pushed the bell, he grabbed the doorknob. He'd known some burglars and they always told him, you'd be amazed at how often that works. The knob turned, and Milo opened the door. There was nobody in sight. Just the suit of armour standing by the stairs, axe raised.

Milo looked to his right. The double doors to the trophy room were closed. He took a deep breath, prayed that Cross wasn't in the room. Prayed that there was no one in there he knew. Then he went in the house, shut the door behind him and crossed to the trophy room.

He turned one door handle and pushed. The door didn't budge. He tried the other handle. That door didn't open either. Milo thought back. In all the times he'd been here Cross had never locked this room. The doors were always either wide open, one of them at least, or they were shut but unlocked and Cross just opened them and walked in. Why would they be locked now? Milo tried each handle again. He tried them one at a time and then together. He shook them and pounded his shoulder against them. Why were they locked? Why? He rattled and banged and threw himself against them again and again. His desperation made the noise not matter. The doors, however, would not open.

Milo backed up several steps. He'd run at the door. Launch himself and burst it open. He'd never done that before. He figured it was something for TV, but he didn't know what else to do. Then, out of the corner

220

of his eye, he saw the armour and the glint of the axe.

He ran across the foyer and grabbed at the handle held in the metal gloves. He tried to pull it free but the gloves held on tightly. He pulled again but that was no more effective than cranking the door handles.

That's when Milo tried lifting the axe up. It moved. He tugged upward again and the axe rose a little further. Milo pulled harder and, hand over hand, he lifted the axe higher and higher. Then it was free of the armoured gloves and in Milo's hands. It was heavier than he'd expected and it fell to the floor with a clang.

He picked it up and held the blade at shoulder height and turned to the double doors. He was trying to figure out which door to hit, and exactly where, when he saw the handle turn. The door opened just enough to show that it was very dark inside, and Cross stepped out. He shut the door again and locked it. Then he turned back to Milo.

"What are you going to do with that?" he asked. "It's easier if you use the key." He held it out between his thumb and forefinger and shook it in Milo's face.

"Let me in there," Milo said.

"I don't think so. I didn't even let you in my house. Get out of here now."

"Stand back," Milo said, then he took a swing with the axe. It felt really good. Whoever made it back in the Dark Ages surely knew his stuff, Milo thought. The weapon was beautifully balanced and it swung like a perfect pendulum. Milo did it again. It made a swish as the blade cut through the air. He took a step forward and swung the axe a third time. "It's really sharp, you know. I could cut off your arm just like that." He lunged forward slightly and swung the axe again, aiming it vaguely at Cross's left arm.

Cross jerked back. "Are you mad?"

"Oooh," Milo said. "There's a thought. Maybe I am." He swung the axe again.

"Put that down and get out of my house." Cross sounded shrill but he still had the voice of a man who was used to having his orders obeyed.

Milo didn't pay any attention. "You never told me the provenance of this thing," Milo said. "But lemme guess. They used to use it to cut the dicks off guys who fucked other men's women." The axe was swinging back and forth like a metronome. Cross's gaze kept drifting back to it like it was a mesmerist's watch - shifting from Milo's face to the blade. Milo pressed forward and Cross backed up the same distance.

"I want in that room," Milo said. Then he pulled the axe back and swung it hard at Cross's belly.

Cross lurched backwards, startled when he hit the wall. The blade sliced by within inches of him. He dropped to the ground and the backswing whistled above his head. Cross pressed himself flat to the shiny floor, his hands grasping the back of his head. He whimpered as Milo lifted the axe high in the air.

"Is Cara in that room?" Milo asked. He thought his voice sounded very soft and calm.

"Yes," Cross said. It sounded like he was sobbing. "Yes. Yes. Cara's in that room."

Milo remembered the most effective technique for chopping wood from summers when he was young. He'd worked on a farm and splintered cord after cord. He knew he was still in good enough shape that he could drive an axe this sharp and this heavy clean through anything, if he swung it properly and if his mind was just as sharply focused.

He held his right hand at the base of the ax handle and his left hand up near the blade. As he brought the axe back over his head he'd slide his left hand down the handle to touch his right, giving him maximum momentum and impact when the axe came up over his head and then down very fast and very hard. Milo knew that, if he did it just right, someone would have to come repair the gouge he left in the hardwood floor. And, of course, a painter would have to be called in, too.

Milo fixed his eyes on the target and began his swing. The handle slipped through his left hand smoothly and he had the axe poised, held high, just ready to drive downward. He felt good. He was perfectly balanced. The target had stopped moving. The axe was steady and his mind was made up. Then he heard a sound behind him that made him change his mind. It was a sound that had made him freeze the first time he heard it. It was instinctive. In the same way that a kitten knows to be afraid of a dog the first time it sees one. And every time since it had the same effect on him.

Someone behind his back had cocked a gun. Milo lowered the axe slowly and turned to look.

"Don't, Milo," Cara said. She was standing in the door of the trophy room, open again.

Milo started to set the axe on the floor, but Cross had risen to his knees and made a tut-tutting noise. "Put your toys back where they belong when you're finished playing with them," he said.

Milo walked over to the stairs and slipped the handle of the axe back into the clutches of the armour.

Milo breathed deeply. He was glad Cara had stopped him from killing Cross. That would have been a tough one to get out of. And he was glad he'd gotten there in time. Glad she was alive.

He started to go over to her. To take the gun from her. So he could cover Cross while she packed and they got the hell out. But she poked the barrel at him, motioning for him to back off. He was startled but he did it. You didn't want to mess with a woman with a gun.

He decided to pretend the weapon wasn't there. "Run upstairs," he said, "and grab a few things. Some jewels or some cash or something. We can catch a flight at the airport. The first thing going anywhere."

But she didn't run upstairs. She didn't grab anything. Instead, she walked over to Cross and handed him the pistol.

Cross lowered the gun, pointing it at the floor. "Would you care for a cognac?" he asked.

Milo didn't want to hang around. He wanted to get the hell out of there and he wanted to take Cara with him. But Cross had a gun in his hand and he was holding it like he really knew what he was doing, and that made Milo cautious.

Then again, after nearly just killing a guy, a cognac would taste pretty good. And maybe in the act of pouring it the rich man would put the gun down. "Yeah. If it's old and expensive, make it a big one."

Cross went to the small bar beside his desk and took up a decanter. Milo had drunk from it before and knew that it was good. But as the rich man took the stopper out of the decanter and raised it and poured into two matching glasses, the gun never left his other hand. Milo settled for Plan B.

He took the cognac. His hand was shaking and he felt all of a sudden weary as the adrenalin left him. He swallowed quickly. The cognac burned all the way down. "Thanks," he said. "I have to go now." He put the glass down, looked at Cara. Then he started to turn for the door. But Cross raised the gun and pointed it at him. Milo froze.

Cross stood by his desk, sipping his drink and holding the outstretched pistol at Milo's stomach. He made it all look very elegant and sophisticated. Like something from a Noel Coward play. "Don't go just yet," he said.

"I got to," Milo said. "I'm parked illegally."

"They don't ticket much in this neighbourhood." Cross began to pour himself more cognac. He held the decanter out to Milo and raised an eyebrow. Milo nodded and Cross poured more for him, too. He motioned with the gun for Milo to pick up his drink.

As Milo did so, he asked, "What calibre is that?"

"It's big enough to hurt you quite badly," Cross said. "Now tell me why you're here."

Milo shrugged. "I thought Cara was in trouble. I thought she needed me."

"Is that it?"

"Yes," Milo said.

Cross moved away from the desk and walked across the room, past Cara, and stood by the fireplace. He set his drink down on the mantel. "What kind of trouble, Milo?"

Milo stared at him and didn't answer.

"It doesn't matter. I know what you thought. Truth to tell, you were in the ballpark. I also know that you wanted my money, very likely that you wanted to live in my house. Well, Milo, part of your wish is about to come true."

"What are you talking about?"

Cross never took his eyes off Milo. "Show him, Cara."

She lifted something off the desk and handed it to Milo. It was a small pile of Polaroid pictures. They were of Milo. He was naked and asleep, the covers pulled back. Every part of his body had been photographed.

"Where did you get these?" he asked. But he knew, and answered his own question. "You took these," he said to Cara.

"Finally, an accurate deduction," Cross said.

Milo looked at him and then beyond him to the wall. He looked at the photographs in his hand again and then at Cara and then at the other heads stuck on the wall and then back at the space above the mantel. "Oh my God. You two knew one another all along."

"Would you care for another cognac?" Cross asked.

Milo shook his head, but it was as much in disbelief as in answer. "Why? Why me?"

"You fit all the criteria. And you're very discreet. I know you've told no one about this. No one will miss you." Cross walked over and took the photographs from Milo's hand. Then he fanned them and gazed down at them. "And you'll look lovely up there," he said softly.

"But why the charade? Why spin it out so long? Why didn't you just kill me and get it over with?"

Cross pointed at a tiger's head on the wall. "I tracked that magnificent creature for four days through the jungles of Sumatra. It was a fascinating experience, seeing what the quarry would do. It was a challenge. I learned much. I know of men who have dug pits in the jungle and covered them over and waited for big cats to fall into them. Then, from the edge of the pit, they shoot. The animal can't run or hide. It's slaughter that does nothing to help those men grow, and I have no respect for them." He waved his hand around the room. "Each of these trophies is hard won. And each of them taught me a great deal about myself and about animal behaviour."

Milo digested this. "So was this a growth experience for you?"

Cross shook his head. "Unfortunately, you did nothing that hadn't been predicted."

Milo sometimes wondered how he would feel at the end of his life. But he had never imagined it quite like this. He imagined being surrounded

by people who cared about him. He imagined tears and death-bed rec-
onciliations and immortal last words. But all he could think to do was
turn to Cara and say, "You told me you loved me."

"Did I?" she replied. "Oh." When she looked at Milo, there was
nothing in her eyes to suggest that they had ever known one another. No
hint that she had whispered to him in the dark.

Milo felt numb with humiliation. He looked at Cross. "You used
her as bait."

"Oh, Milo, what a pathetic detective you are. You still don't get it,
do you?" Cross gave him a cold smile. "She wasn't the bait," he said. "I
was. And it was all her idea."

Milo looked at Cara's blank face and could think of nothing more
to say.

Publishing History

Boogie Man

Originally published as "A Difference of Degree" in *Mike Shayne Mystery Magazine*, August, 1985.

Reprinted in *Northern Frights*, edited by Don Hutchison, Mosaic Press, 1992.

Recorded on audio tape as part of *Northern Frights*, read by R.H. Thomson, Tangled Web Audio, 1996.

Dead Meet

Originally published in *Cold Blood III*, Mosaic Press, 1990.

This One's Trouble

Originally published in *Alfred Hitchcock's Mystery Magazine,* July, 1991.

Finalist for the Crime Writers of Canada's Arthur Ellis Award for Best Short Story, 1992.

Bush Fever

Originally published in *Cold Blood III* as by Jack Paris, Mosaic Press, 1990.

Reprinted in *Secret Tales of the Arctic Trails*, edited by David Skene-Melvin, Simon and Pierre, 1997.

Whistling Past the Graveyard
> Originally published in *Criminal Shorts*, edited by Eric Wright
> and Howard Engel, Macmillan, 1992.
> Reprinted in *Ellery Queen Mystery Magazine,* May, 1993.

The Vampires Next Door
> Originally published as "Imposter" in *Northern Frights III*,
> edited by Don Hutchison, Mosaic Press, 1995.

Bombed
> Originally published in *Ellery Queen Mystery Magazine,*
> June, 1994.
> Reprinted in *Bloody York*, edited by David Skene-Melvin,
> Simon and Pierre, 1996.

Last Resort
> Originally published in *Cold Blood IV*, Mosaic Press, 1992.